ASHE Higher Education Report: Volume 33, Number 2
Kelly Ward, Lisa E. Wolf-Wendel, Series Editors

D1278309

Christian Faith and Scholarship: An Exploration of Contemporary Developments

Todd C. Ream
Perry L. Glanzer

Christian Faith and Scholarship: An Exploration of Contemporary Developments
Todd C. Ream and Perry L. Glanzer
ASHE Higher Education Report: Volume 33, Number 2
Kelly Ward, Lisa E. Wolf-Wendel, Series Editors

ISSN 1551-6970   electronic ISSN 1554-6306   ISBN 978-04702-28890

The ASHE Higher Education Report is part of the Jossey-Bass Higher and Adult Education Series and is published six times a year by Wiley Subscription Services, Inc., A Wiley Company, at Jossey-Bass, 989 Market Street, San Francisco, California 94103-1741.

For subscription information, see the Back Issue/Subscription Order Form in the back of this volume.

CALL FOR PROPOSALS: Prospective authors are strongly encouraged to contact Kelly Ward (kaward@wsu.edu) or Lisa Wolf-Wendel (lwolf@ku.edu). See "About the ASHE Higher Education Report Series" in the back of this volume.

Visit the Jossey-Bass Web site at **www.josseybass.com.**

Printed in the United States of America on acid-free recycled paper.

The ASHE Higher Education Report is indexed in CIJE: Current Index to Journals in Education (ERIC), Current Abstracts (EBSCO), Education Index/Abstracts (H.W. Wilson), ERIC Database (Education Resources Information Center), Higher Education Abstracts (Claremont Graduate University), IBR & IBZ: International Bibliographies of Periodical Literature (K.G. Saur), Resources in Education (ERIC)

Advisory Board

The ASHE Higher Education Report Series is sponsored by the Association for the Study of Higher Education (ASHE), which provides an editorial advisory board of ASHE members.

Contents

Executive Summary

Despite many predictions to the contrary, religion remains a powerful force in both American society and the world at large. Because of this power, it also remains a disconcerting reality for many individuals in higher education. Scholarship that incorporates religious faith as a valued and important perspective is thought at times to reduce the sense of objective inquiry modern manifestations of scholarship were supposed to uphold and embody. Historically, scholars used this ideal to marginalize religion from the scholarly conversation during much of modernity. Nonetheless, as Mark U. Edwards notes, "Not mentioning religious (or analogous) convictions does not make them go away" (2006, p. 2). Religious faith has not only failed to go away but has also regained a place among other valued and informed perspectives brought to bear on scholarly practices.

In this monograph we recognize with Alan Wolfe that "religion is here to stay" and that the "form it takes and how it will continue to interact with culture and politics is very much open to discussion" (2004, p. 6). Numerous scholars have joined this discussion. We believe that both understanding and continuing this conversation are vitally important for higher education's own critical self-reflection. The scholarly debates we describe in this monograph are rarely given attention by a media culture that reduces debates about religion and education to school board arguments over evolution or the displaying of a cross in a college chapel. Instead of focusing on the headline-grabbing issues, this work summarizes and adds to an emerging but less well-known scholarly conversation about the relationship shared between religion and scholarship in the academy. We hope it helps readers set aside fears and stereotypes associated with conversations about religion in public and academic life. As Wolfe notes, "Much of the new scholarship on religion enables Americans to recognize that a revival of religion need not lead to the creation of a theocracy or that the religious conflict so evident around the world need not be played out within the United States" (2004, p. 6). Likewise, a revival of the type of conversation about religion and scholarship we describe should not be judged a priori as a threat to scholarship, especially in higher education where new theoretical exploration and increased understanding are valued.

To introduce readers to the current conversation, we address five major topics: the history of secularization in American higher education and scholarship; the general models of faith and scholarship in various Christian traditions; the ways that individual scholars, networks, and institutions approach the question of religious faith and scholarship; the concerns such a question raises for academic freedom; and the relationship between religious faith and scholarship in what we identify as the larger tournament of narratives. Overall, we seek to chronicle how religious scholars and institutions of higher education are now writing their own postmodern narratives about the future of religion in higher education.

Foreword

"Some ideas are bigger than our intellectual capacity to deal with them. Some news is richer than the words we have to describe it. When that happens, we turn gratefully to art and music and works of the imagination. That's why on Easter we put the emphasis on beautiful hymns and great organ and trumpet music. Words alone cannot convey the message," writes John M. Buchanan, editor of *The Christian Century* (2007, p. 3). As a member of the Fourth Presbyterian Church of Chicago where Buchanan is the senior pastor, my fellow members and I know first hand that if anyone can describe something or an idea with accuracy and insight, he can.

When authors try to write about religion and faith, which is fundamentally transcendent in its nature, we have a challenge. We also have a problem in the academy, as Stanley Fish recently wrote in the *New York Times:* "The truth claims of a religion—at least of religions like Christianity, Judaism and Islam—are not incidental to its identity: they *are* its identity" (2007, p. A27). Words cannot adequately or at least not fully describe the essence of the topic. It is like trying to measure the immeasurable—it is not possible.

That is why I welcome a book such as this one in the ASHE series. It is not the typical topic of an ASHE book, as it deals with a review of matters of religion and not summaries of social and educational research. It is more abstract and to many of us will be quite obtuse, given our desire for concrete and pragmatic approaches to fixing and problem solving.

But most important, it is a book about what is to be considered the true and the good, something that the academy has not dealt with with much enthusiasm in the last few decades, as Sharon Parks (2000) points out in her argument for having the university become a mentoring community for the development of an adult critical faith. In my summary of the research on the religious development of students during college (2007), students do not merely and uniformly become more secular.

Recently a number of faculty and scholars, including the two authors of this book, argued that the Enlightenment no longer has its powerful grip on the academy. Postmodern and postsecular worldviews are now powerful competitors in the marketplace of ideas and perspectives. "Rational choice" theory no longer is regarded as being able to explain all of human behavior. John Sommerville, in his critique of the American research university with its foundation grounded in secularism, argues that these places of scholarship have become irrelevant. They are truncated institutions because they fail to "connect with the human being's deepest interests and most pressing concerns" (2006, p. 9)

This is a book that any reader will react to emotionally as well as intellectually. Faith is deeply personal but not private. We need to have good scholarship about religion and faith, recognizing that faith and the practice of faith represent two different but closely connected realms. The authors of this monograph, Todd Ream and Perry Glanzer, thus have a huge task before them—to present the arguments from their worldview, which is Christian, in ways that will invite a conversation about the scholarship of religion rather than be a conversation stopper, the most likely situation in the academy today (Rorty, 1999).

From my vantage, they do a commendable job. The reader, it is hoped, will become engaged in the topic and disagree with the arguments put forth by these "biased" authors but be more informed about the issues. It is not easy reading—the topic is not an easy one—but it is perhaps one of the most important for the academy to once again really get serious about. I wish you well in your venture.

Larry A. Braskamp
Loyola University

Acknowledgments

To rightfully offer thanks to all those individuals who helped make such a monograph possible is a tall task indeed. We are the beneficiaries of educational communities and families who have graciously sacrificed much to help us succeed. The strengths of our efforts were improved as a result of their commitment to us as friends, colleagues, and loved ones, while any shortcomings are invariably of our own doing.

Todd Ream would first like to thank Lauren Sheehan. With great attention to detail, Lauren provided much-needed assistance in tracking down sources and reading through the details of this manuscript. Second, I would like to thank the staff of the Jackson Library and, in particular, Lynn Crawford. In these friends and colleagues, I find not only great hospitality but also valued partners in the endeavor of scholarship. Third, I would like to thank Jerry Pattengale for his patience and his support. Despite the heavy administrative responsibilities he carries at Indiana Wesleyan University, Jerry always makes time for his friends and colleagues. In many ways, he embodies how the highest of commitments to collegiality and scholarship can transform a community. Finally, my greatest debt of gratitude goes to my wife, Sara Ream. Without her love and support, I would lack the persistence needed to complete such a project. Through the years, she has always been there for me. She believed in me at times when I wondered whether I believed in myself. The efforts present in these pages are but small ways of saying "thank you" for all she has done for me.

Perry Glanzer thanks Baylor University and the School of Education for the summer sabbatical that allowed the completion of this project. I appreciate the leadership at Baylor University and its support of efforts to explore the integration of faith and scholarship. Without Baylor's commitment to that vision, works such as this one would not be possible. I would also like to thank my graduate assistants, Jennette Walkine and Claudiu Cimpean, for their tireless help with formatting the references and rereading the entire manuscript. Most of all, I would like to thank my wife, Rhonda, who demonstrates in her life of sacrificial love, care, and service the virtues that characterize the religious life of the heart that scholarship can only describe but not produce.

In the end, we dedicate this monograph to Addison Ream, Ashley Ream, Bennett Glanzer, and Cody Glanzer. In the hearts and minds of our children, we are reminded of the need for places, practices, and ultimately people who see religious faith and scholarly work as part of a larger effort to understand what it means to be truly human.

Published online in Wiley InterScience
(www.interscience.wiley.com) • DOI: 10.1002/aehe.3302

A False Prophet?

IN 1882, THE SON OF A LUTHERAN MINISTER published what some considered a prophetic book. The author, however, did not take the traditional prophetic role of warning people about God's impending judgment. Instead, in Friedrich Nietzsche's *The Gay Science* (1882/1974), we meet the figure of a Madman who runs into the marketplace shouting, "I seek God! I seek God!" only to have his cultured despisers respond with the now often quoted, "God is dead. God remains dead. And we have killed him" (p. 181). In light of developments regarding the relationship between religion and scholarship in the following twentieth century, some scholars claimed the cultured despisers proved to be secular prophets. Even recently, Catholic scholar James Turner observed, "There is . . . , I believe, a scholarly culture that tends to assume that religion is a dead force intellectually: that its traditions, however interesting as objects of study for historians or anthropologists, do not speak to live issues in scholarship today" (2002, p. 20). Unlike Turner, others have even celebrated the supposed demise of religion and joined with Nietzsche in proclaiming, "We have left the land and embarked. We have burned our bridges behind us—indeed, we have gone farther and destroyed the land behind us" (1882/1974, p. 180).

Emerging evidence in the twenty-first century suggests, however, that Nietzsche was perhaps a false prophet. In fact, the recent death of a contemporary philosopher prompted announcements of God's resurrection in the academy. "When Jacques Derrida died," Stanley Fish (2005) recently wrote, "I was called by a reporter who wanted to know what would succeed high theory and the triumvirate of race, gender, and class as the center of intellectual energy in the academy. I answered like a shot: religion" (p. 1). Although theology is unlikely to ever reassert itself in a comprehensive sense as the queen of the sciences, if Fish is correct, Nietzsche may have overestimated the degree to which we obliterated the land behind us.

Certainly the turn of the twenty-first century has seen religious faith reemerge at least to some point of influence in relation to scholarship. A sample of recent publications reveals how the discussion in higher education in relation to matters of religious faith is shifting. As part of their larger Spirituality in Higher Education project, scholars at UCLA's Higher Education Research Institute released a report in spring 2006 entitled "Spirituality and the Professorate"; the cover of the March/April 2006 issue of *Change* magazine bears the title "Religion in the Academy"; and the spring/summer 2006 issue of *The Hedgehog Review* includes a collection of essays all falling under the larger title of "After Secularization." Paul Dovre noted, in a recent volume on religion in higher education, "There is today more discussion about the role of religion in the academy than at any time in the past forty years and more commitment to the project of Christian higher education than there was just ten years ago" (2002, p. ix).

In light of these developments and the robust contemporary discussion about religion and scholarship in the academy, this monograph offers an overview of the various ways conversations about religion and religiously informed scholarship are increasing among scholars in secular and church-related colleges and universities. Specifically, it addresses the history of secularization in American higher education and scholarship, the general models of faith and scholarship in dominant religious traditions, the ways that individual scholars, networks, and institutions approach the question of religious faith and scholarship, the concerns such a question raises for academic freedom, and the relationship between religious faith and scholarship in what we identify as the larger tournament of narratives.

At the heart of this monograph is the debate over how educational institutions and individual scholars define and identify quality scholarship. Each year, tenure and promotion committees contend with the issue of not only how to define scholarship but also how to evaluate it. The modern research university that arose around the turn of the twentieth century forged a general consensus that scholarship was the discovery of new knowledge as refereed by a jury of peers. Implicit in this definition of scholarship was the belief that modern forms of epistemology called for an application of an objective form of reason. Such a form of reason was to be free from various manifestations of subjective bias such as religious faith. On an institutional level, religious faith came to be the prerogative of various volunteer associations both on and off campus. On an individual level, many scholars who identified themselves as religious found ways to set their faith aside from their scholarly efforts. As a result, a lack of clarity emerged concerning what unique contribution church-related colleges and universities and religious scholars might offer the larger scholarly world. Toward the end of the 1960s, analysts of higher education such as Christopher Jencks and David Riesman (2002/1968) even called into question whether church-related colleges and universities, Protestant schools in particular, would survive in any significant sense.

Both the definition of scholarship and the fortunes of religious scholars, colleges, and universities have changed. Ernest Boyer (1990), perhaps influenced by his Christian convictions (see Jacobsen and Jacobsen, 2004, pp. 48–54), attempted to broaden the definition of scholarship beyond the discovery of new knowledge alone to include the scholarship of integration, application, and teaching. Although Boyer's attempt to add these components to the definition of scholarship is commendable, the definition we employ in our monograph is what Boyer would label "the scholarship of discovery." We recognize the validity of the other forms of scholarship that Boyer recognizes, but the scholarship of discovery is the form of scholarship generated by the rise of the research university at the turn of the twentieth century. As a result, the most advanced discussion of the place of religious faith in relation to scholarship comes in terms of the relationship it shares with this particular form.

Part of what we demonstrate in this monograph is that even within this form of scholarship, the demand for an application of objective reason was altered to recognize that reason can be informed by what were once considered more subjective qualities such as religion. In many cases, the identity of the scholar went from being deemed a corrupting influence to being deemed an essential and inescapable component. The turn of the twentieth century witnessed the displacement of religious faith as the academy's metanarrative and the reassertion of religious faiths in the academy's larger tournament of narratives. One can find scholars such as Robert J. Nash (2001) now arguing for the need to initiate conversations in both public and private nonsectarian universities concerning the relationship between scholarship and religious faith.

At the institutional level, this change has also strengthened the distinctive contribution of church-related colleges and universities and has perhaps increased their visibility. For instance, contrary to Jencks and Riesman's predictions of a demise in Protestant colleges and universities, member institutions of the largely Protestant Council for Christian Colleges and Universities (CCCU) grew 36.9 percent between 1990 and 1998 versus 13.4 percent for other private universities and 3 percent for public universities (Council for Christian Colleges and Universities, 2001). When one looks at enrollment trends from 1990 to 2004, CCCU institutions grew 70.6 percent versus 28 percent for other private universities and 12.8 percent for public universities (Green, 2005). Although no one can likely identify the level of correlation between such changes, a historical one exists nonetheless.

A second conceptual theme in this monograph concerns the postmodern discussion of narratives and metanarratives initiated by Jean-François Lyotard. Lyotard uses the word *modern* to describe any science that justifies itself by "making an explicit appeal to some grant narrative, such as the dialectics of Spirit, the hermeneutics of meaning, the emancipation of the rational or working subject, or the creation of wealth" (1984, p. xxiii). Contained in these narratives is a philosophy of history that helps to justify a particular approach to knowledge.

Before the turn of the twentieth century, religious faith was the metanarrative that proved definitive in American culture. In relation to scholarly efforts at many church-related institutions, religious faith may still possess a privileged position in relation to other narratives—perhaps even bordering on being classified once again as a metanarrative. In the twentieth century a secular, empirical form of reason embodied in modern science took Christian theology's place.

According to Lyotard, one of the definitive components of postmodernity is incredulity toward any metanarratives, or the unwillingness of individuals to acknowledge that any singular narrative (or metanarrative) is held in higher esteem than another. In particular, postmodernity in this sense calls into question the ability of reason and science to be applied in a universal sense by any particular scholar or institution. Although the new postmodern culture and its understanding of narratives now reopens a position for religious narratives, that culture also no longer recognizes the place of a metanarrative. Consequently, in the postmodern academy one tension that inevitably arises involves the relationship that religious narratives share with other narratives among not only the institutional cultures of church-related colleges and universities but also among scholars throughout the academy. As a result, an important debate now exists over how institutions or particular scholars can argue for religious faith to serve in a metanarrative-like capacity when such a capacity has ceased to be recognized in the larger culture. This monograph aims to show how religious scholars and institutions in higher education address this challenge.

The Secularization of Scholarship in American Higher Education

IN THE INTRODUCTION TO HIS BOOK, *The Outrageous Idea of Christian Scholarship*, George Marsden begins by asking some provocative questions about the role of religion in the academy: "Why are there in mainstream academia almost no identifiable Christian schools of thought to compare with various Marxist, feminist, gay, post-modern, African-American, conservative or liberal schools of thought? If one compares for example, the number of Marxists in America with the number of Christians, the disparity in their visibility in mainstream academia is truly remarkable. What is it about the dominant academic culture that teaches people they must suppress reflection on the intellectual implications of their faith?" (1997, p. 6). Marsden's observations about the secularization of scholarship in America are especially puzzling, considering that many of the schools of thought he mentions have no colleges or universities while there are more than four hundred church-related colleges and universities in America.

Of course, the answer to these questions lies in the history of American higher education. In fact, Marsden's own puzzlement with the answers to these questions led him to write one of the first major scholarly works discussing the secularization of American higher education, *The Soul of the American University: From Protestant Establishment to Established Nonbelief* (1994). He notes in the introduction to this work: "Since it is nowhere written in stone that the highest sort of human intellectual activity must exclude religious perspectives, it is helpful, I think, to consider how it came to pass that so many academics believe that such exclusions are part of the definition of their task" (p. 7).

Marsden's groundbreaking work and a number of other works have added to our understanding of this past. Thus this chapter offers an overview of recent scholarship concerning the secularization of American higher education as well as the contemporary controversy about the theory of secularization in general and the secularization of scholarship in particular. To accomplish these tasks, we first consider various definitions and understandings of secularization and clarify what we mean when discussing the secularization of scholarship. Second, we outline recent works that address the secularization of scholarship in American higher education and how their authors understand the origins of the secularization of scholarship. Finally, we summarize recent discussions about the inevitably of secularization, particularly in scholarship, and its relationship to the possibility of scholarship informed by faith perspectives.

The Secularization of American Higher Education
Defining Secularization
C. John Sommerville (1998) provides an insightful overview of the five understandings of secularization employed by scholars. When discussing secularization scholars may refer to the secularization of society, institutions, activities, populations, or mentalities or some combination of these five.

In the context of higher education, it is possible to identify examples of each type. When addressing the secularization of societies, secularization refers to "the separation of religious activities, groups or ideas from others characteristic of the society" (p. 250). For instance, societies become secularized when the government separates itself from church-related institutions and no longer identifies with a particular confession or funds it. For example, the early American states that disestablished their churches secularized in this manner (moves that also influenced the colleges within the states). This type of secularization is often understood as a particular form of what sociologists refer to as "institutional differentiation" (Casanova, 1994).

The second type of secularization, the institutional form, involves "the transformation of an institution that had once been considered religious in character into something not thought of as religious . . . like the European university . . ." (p. 250). In higher education this transformation occurs when a particular college or university separates itself from church governance and financial support and excludes Christian purposes from its mission (Burtchaell, 1998; Marsden, 1994).Both societal and institutional forms of secularization are captured in Webster's dictionary (1978) definition of the term—"the separation, as of civil and educational affairs, from religious or ecclesiastical influence or control."

Third, some scholars use the word *secularization* in reference to particular activities either as a whole or at particular institutions. For example, the activity of higher education as a whole may be secularized (it becomes largely a state or professional function rather than a church function). Such secularization also involves an internal secularization of educational activities involving the university's rituals, curriculum, and ethos (Burtchaell, 1998; Marsden, 1994; Marsden and Longfield, 1992).

Universities no longer mandate attendance at chapel, drop religious requirements for entrance, and no longer require Bible or theology courses. Perhaps the Bible department even changes its name to "religious studies." Fourth, some scholars use the word *secularization* to describe changes in religious beliefs and behaviors of a particular population such as faculty and students. Perhaps fewer believe in God, attend church, or pray. Finally, the fifth version, the secularization of mentalities, refers more to a general, perhaps even unconscious, shift in worldview that occurs when individuals or scholars "look upon the world and their own lives without the benefit of religious interpretations" (Berger, 1967, p. 108). For instance, scholars may believe in God and even claim to support various other religious beliefs, but they undertake most of their lives and almost all of their professional scholarly work without reference to such beliefs. In *The Secularization of the European Mind in the Nineteenth Century,* for example, Owen Chadwick focuses on this aspect when he claims that secularization is a growing propensity of humanity "to do without religion" (1975, p. 16). This fifth version of secularization also appears to be the one to which Nietzsche refers and the one that Marsden was most concerned about in the introductory quote. It is also this version that is the major focus of this monograph.

Many scholars of course use some combination of these understandings, often without distinguishing between them. For instance, in his *History of*

Christianity 1650–1950: Secularization of the West, James Nichols (1956) describes secularization as "emancipation both from clerical control and from a religious orientation" (p. 10). As we will see, scholars addressing the history of the secularization of American higher education also tend to use a combination of these meanings. (And we recognize that all these different forms of secularization may work together.)

Nonetheless, some versions of secularization can and do occur in isolation. For instance, using the fifth understanding of secularization, a scholar could practice his or her craft in the academy, hold religious convictions or consider himself or herself spiritual (he or she has not secularized according to version four), and perhaps even work in a religious college funded and governed by a religious denomination (version two) where chapel is held regularly (version three). His or her religious convictions could remain differentiated from his or her professional life, however, and not be woven into the fabric of questions to be pursued as part of one's scholarly work. In fact a scholar could support spirituality in higher education (Astin and Astin, 2006) with regard to teaching, service, or student development and still exhibit a secular approach to scholarship in his or her research practices. Moreover, many scholars we will discuss in this monograph are now attempting to reverse or restrain this fifth aspect of secularization while not necessarily advocating the recovery of religious practices such as chapel at state universities (version 1) or the re-Christianization of secularized private universities such as Harvard or Princeton (version 2).

The Religious Roots of American Higher Education

The roots of the vast majority of early American colleges and universities lie in religious and not secular soil. The longest history of institutions of higher learning in the United States belongs to colleges and universities related to denominations that today fall under the category of mainline Protestantism. For example, Harvard University (1636), Yale University (1701), and Dartmouth College (1769) were established by Congregationalists. The College of William and Mary (1693) and Columbia University (1754) were established by Anglicans. Princeton University (1746) was established by Presbyterians. Other denominational schools included in the category of mainline Protestantism would be those started by Baptists (American), Brethren, the Disciples of Christ, Lutherans (Evangelical Lutheran Church in America), Quakers, and United Methodists (Cuninggim, 1994).

In addition, what today would be called "evangelical Protestantism" also played an important role in these early colleges. Historians trace the origins of evangelicalism to a group of mid-eighteenth century leaders in these churches such as George Whitefield, John Wesley, Jonathan Edwards, and Nicholas zon Zinzendorf, who attempted to revitalize European and North American Protestant churches, what we call mainline Protestant denominations (Noll, 1994; Bebbington, 1989). These evangelical reformers emphasized the importance of "conversionism (an emphasis on the 'new birth' as a life-changing religious experience), biblicism (a reliance on the Bible as ultimate religious authority), activism (a concern for sharing the faith), and crucicentrism (a focus on Christ's redeeming work on the cross)" (Noll, 1994, p. 8).

Before the Civil War, evangelical Protestants such as Jonathan Edwards and Timothy Dwight often led or participated in many early American colleges, among them Princeton and Yale (Noll, 1994). Evangelicals also started numerous colleges, including Dartmouth, Amherst, Oberlin, Wesleyan, and Wheaton. At times it might be hard to distinguish between evangelical and mainline Protestant schools, as numerous schools were founded by denominations that would have been influenced by thinkers and individuals who could be identified as being from both traditions. Evangelicals often operated within mainline Protestantism, so it is difficult to define them according to particular denominations. Nonetheless, today some contemporary schools in the category include many Southern Baptist, Assemblies of God, Lutheran (Missouri Synod), Presbyterian (Presbyterian Church in America), and Wesleyan (Free Methodist Church and the Wesleyan Church) institutions. Like mainline Protestantism, smaller groups such as the Quakers, the Brethren, and the Reformed have schools identifying themselves with evangelical Protestantism. Evangelical Protestantism is also populated with a host of nondenominational churches and thus several nondenominational colleges and universities.

Although the Catholic tradition of higher education in Europe reaches back to the origins of universities and includes early thinkers such as Thomas Aquinas and the well-known theologian and theorist of higher education John Henry Newman, Catholics were initially considered outsiders to an American education system dominated by mainline Protestants (Carpenter, 2002; Gleason, 1995). Nonetheless, various Catholic orders such as the Augustinians, the Benedictines, the Congregation of the Holy Cross, the Dominicans, the Franciscans, and the Jesuits established a wide variety of colleges and universities in America, including Georgetown University (1789), Fordham University (1841), the University of Notre Dame (1842), Villanova University (1842), and the College of the Holy Cross (1843).

All these colleges at one time had strong financial and leadership connections with their sponsoring denomination or religious order. Required religious courses such as Bible and theology also ensured that religion influenced the curriculum. Moreover, the religious ethos permeated the rules and rituals of the schools (Marsden, 1994; Burtchaell, 1998). Yet as James Nichols (1956) observes, the history of Western education starting from the seventeenth century saw a gradual secularization: "Instead of being a preparation for man's communion with God, education came to be dominated by utilitarian motives and political preoccupations, both disciplined by 'natural' rather than Christian morality. . . . Theological instruction and worship, meanwhile, have occupied an ever smaller place in the curriculum, and their relevance to other subjects of study has been ever less obvious" (p. 10).

The secularization of scholarship played an important role in this movement.

The Secularization of Scholarship

The work of Thomas Albert Howard offers a helpful intellectual history of the secularization of academic scholarship. In his book entitled *Religion and the Rise of Historicism,* Howard (2000) contends that intellectual secularization originated in the German academy—particularly between theology and the emerging discipline of history. Methods dominating disciplines apart from theology such as science and history began to take their place in the academy. For example, "history became an autonomous *Wissenschaft,* and perspectives and methods drawn from history began to affect other areas of inquiry, notably theology and biblical criticism" (p. 2). As a result, historical consciousness not only became independent of theology but also began to demand that truth claims in theology conform to its means of determining validity.

In *Protestant Theology and the Making of the Modern German University,* Howard (2006) expands this story beyond the purview of historical consciousness. He describes how political ends and methods further reduced the influence of Christian theology. In particular, "by promoting confessional harmony, emphasizing critical scholarship over apologetic, standardizing and mandating state-run accrediting procedures, and maintaining a firm grip on hiring procedures, the [Prussian] state managed to exercise tremendous influence over the religious sphere in society in general" (p. 26). Underlying this shift in influence was the spirit of German idealism. Frederick C. Beiser (2002) describes German Idealism as "the philosophical doctrines initiated by [Immanuel] Kant, and then continued by [J. G.] Fichte, [F.W.J.] Schelling, and [G.W.F.] Hegel" (p. vii). Howard contends that as a philosophical movement "German idealism, in effect, magnified the state as a cultural and ethical force . . . and subordinated the church to the state's own quasi-sacral purposes" (pp. 225–226). Culminating in the work of Hegel, the state, in contrast to the Church, became the institution that embodied humanity's highest ideals. The result is that not only did the state gain control over universities (the first and second types of secularization) but its interests also influenced the degree to which academic scholarship considered theological and religious perspectives (the fifth type).

By virtue of Europe's role in many ways as the intellectual parent of the United States, the secularization impulse inevitably crossed the Atlantic and made its way into the American academy. A great wave of scholarly attention concerning the secularization of American higher education emerged in the 1990s. Marsden's major work on the subject (1994) chronicles the process of secularization in all its forms as it took hold in institutions such as Yale University, Harvard University, Princeton University, The Johns Hopkins University, the University of Michigan, and the University of California, Berkeley. With regard to scholarship, he observes that in the early American system of colleges and universities, Protestant Christianity played a vital role. But "by the 1920s the evangelical Protestantism of the old-time colleges had been effectively excluded from leading university classrooms" (1994, p. 4).

Scholars note that one reason for the exclusion of evangelical Protestantism was the split between Protestants regarding their response to modernity and its various points of pressure—mainline Protestantism being far more receptive to modernity and evangelicals being more likely to reject aspects of modernity. By modernity, scholars usually mean the approach to knowledge fostered in the late nineteenth and twentieth centuries that elevated reason, particularly the inductive method, as the best way to attain reliable knowledge (Marsden, 1994; Sloan, 1994). Louis Dupré suggests that "rational objectivity, moral tolerance, and individual choice as cultural absolutes" define modernity (1993, p. 1). For religious institutions and groups, it resulted in the pressure to accommodate forms of theological methodology to the emerging methodologies of secular history and naturalistic science.

When studying in Germany, many American mainline Protestants imbibed "a historic mandate to pursue truth wherever it might lead, even if it led to unsettling conclusions" (Howard, 2006, p. 330). These scholars brought this mandate back to American colleges and universities related to Protestant denominations. In contrast to mainline Protestants who tended to accept modernism, evangelical Protestants were often sweepingly dismissive of modernity and the scientific naturalism that worked its way into the colleges and universities of mainline Protestantism. Although not all evangelical Protestants are Fundamentalists, Fundamentalism had an important influence in evangelical Protestantism (Noll, 1994). According to Marsden (1980), "Fundamentalism was a loose, diverse, and changing federation of co-belligerents united by their fierce opposition to modernist attempts to bring Christianity into line with modern thought" (p. 4).

Both groups gained an advantage but also paid a price for their approach to modernity. Evangelicals were often forced out of mainline institutions, so they proceeded to found their own schools, allowing many of evangelical Protestantism's colleges and universities to avoid the tide of secularization that slowly found its way to mainline Protestantism's colleges and universities. On the other hand, many young evangelical Protestant colleges and universities were the victims of what Mark Noll in *The Scandal of the Evangelical Mind* identifies as an "intellectual sterility" produced by Fundamentalism. "Under its midwifery, the evangelical community gave birth to virtually no insights into how, under God, the natural world proceeded, how human societies worked, why human nature acted the way it did, or what constituted the blessings and perils of culture" (p. 137). Instead, institutions started to preserve evangelical views; Wheaton College during the 1800s, for example, "found its identity by fighting against the mainstream" (Marsden, 1980, p. 29). In terms of scholarship, the ventures of Fundamentalists were more often warnings "to the general Christian public than a scholarly grappling with the roots of modernism" (Hatch, 1989, p. 215).

Mainline Protestants benefited from their accommodation to modernity by retaining an influence in the universities they established and continued to maintain. This accommodation to historicism and scientific naturalism would eventually come with a price to be paid, however, and some would argue that the compromises mainline Protestants made with modernity ultimately led to the secularization of their colleges and universities (Benne, 2001; Marsden, 1994; Sloan, 1994). As time progressed, university leaders decided that even "liberal Protestantism itself should be moved to the periphery to which other religious perspectives had been relegated for some time" (Marsden, 1994, p. 5).

With regard to the secularization of scholarship, Douglas Sloan (1994) tells one of the most extensive stories. In his book *Faith and Knowledge: Mainline Protestantism and American Higher Education,* he argues that thinkers in the mainline Protestant traditions eventually realized they needed to address the growing monopoly of scientific methods on claims to legitimate knowledge. Some attempted to argue "that affirmations of faith could have roots in knowable reality" (Sloan, 2002, p. 10), but most thinkers in this tradition eventually adopted what Sloan labels the two-realm theory of truth.

"This is the view that on the one side there are the truths of knowledge as these are given predominantly by science and discursive, empirical reason. On the other side are the truths of faith, religious experience, morality, meaning, and value. The latter are seen as grounded not in knowledge but variously in feeling, ethical action, communal convention, folk tradition, or unfathomable mystical experience" (1994, p. ix).

The results of the two-realm theory, Sloan argues, proved disastrous for religion in the academy. He concludes, "This two-realm theory of truth effectively undermined the theological foundation for engagement with the university and set the stage for the collapse of church engagement with the university in the late 1960s" (2002, p. 10).

Part of the sociological basis for the two-realm theory of truth, Mark U. Edwards writes in *Religion on Our Campuses: A Professor's Guide to Communities, Conflicts, and Promising Conversations* (2006), stemmed from the emerging departmental structures in universities that served to reinforce the two-realm theory of truth.

> *Research became "departmentalized." This meant that specialists, including those who were personally religious, came increasingly to believe that religious perspectives or considerations did not belong in disciplinary work. They were not part of the discipline's appropriate subject matter or method, however much they might infuse the scholar's private life or give meaning and background to the work he did as a disciplinary scholar (i.e., give a sense of vocation to his disciplinary work). As fields took form and divided up the expanse of human knowledge, religion was given its own acres but was no longer—except perhaps in grand metaphysical terms—seen as the universal cynosure that made sense of all. That role was now taken, more likely than not, by science, or at least the "scientific method" and the ideal of "objective" naturalistic scholarship [p. 52].*

In other words, although a scholar could be quite a devoted member of a particular religious tradition, the devotion and its experiences were not related to the conversation of how he or she applied empirical reason in the library or the laboratory. In fact, such a scholar may even study religion or religious phenomena.

Ultimately, many scholars lay on mainline Protestantism much of the blame for failing to maintain productive, engaging, and critical understandings of how religion should relate to modern scholarship. Sloan (1994) notes with apparent exasperation, "They even gave up the critical task of showing the problems presented by an exclusively quantitative and instrumental rationalism in providing an adequate understanding of the world of nature itself, much less of the worlds of the spirit" (p. 213). Sloan himself sees a number of weaknesses with this approach. For example, he claims it perpetuated the dualism that characterizes modern ways of approaching knowledge (for example, object-subject, fact-value, public-private, theory-practice) and resulted in the two realms' being viewed unequally, with scientific knowledge understood as being more real. Others argue that the two-realm theory also led to the secularization of mainline educational institutions (Lyon and Beaty, 1999). We believe it is also one of the reasons that, as we will show in the next chapter, traditions outside mainline Protestantism have provided the most important critiques of modern approaches to knowledge as well as the stimulus for the current renaissance regarding religion and scholarship (Benne, 2001).

The Unique Catholic Story

As we will discuss in the next chapter, the main competing intellectual tradition with mainline Protestantism, Roman Catholicism, found ways to resist the two-realm theory of knowledge and some forms of the secularization of scholarship. Yet it also experienced the effects of secularization in an institutional manner that would influence scholarship at Catholic institutions. The work of Philip Gleason (1995) is the definitive volume chronicling secularization in leading Catholic colleges and universities. Instead of speaking directly of secularization, Gleason prefers to speak of the marginalization of the church (the second form of secularization). In an earlier work Gleason (1987) writes about how Catholics in the United States came to conceive of the church as one of any number of social institutions in one's life rather than the definitive social institution. Gleason claims that "the most drastic result of this kind of marginalization—and what makes it psychologically distressing—is that it threatens religious faith by seeming to relativize it" (1987, p. 6). Initially, Gleason established this line of thought in relation to the Catholicism in the United States as a whole in his work entitled *Keeping the Faith: American Catholicism Past and Present* (1987). Gleason later applied this view to how Catholic colleges and universities responded to varying pressures applied by modernity and what he calls "Americanism" in *Contending with Modernity: Catholic Higher Education in the Twentieth Century* (1995).

Catholic colleges and universities struggled with Americanism as they sought to answer questions such as to what end do Catholic colleges and universities prepare graduates—service to the growing American republic or service to the Catholic Church? The other challenge, modernism, Gleason describes "as a many faceted effort to accommodate Catholic teaching to the 'collective change in mentality' taking place in the late nineteenth century, and it raised new questions about many aspects of Catholic doctrine" (1995, p. 12). These aspects of Catholic doctrine included matters as fundamental as the sacraments, Biblical inspiration, and the origins of the church. The accommodations many officials at Catholic colleges and universities eventually made in the face of modernity have proved comparable to those made by officials at Protestant colleges and universities in the face of scientific naturalism (Morey and Piderit, 2006).

The Reasons for the Secularization of Scholarship

Whereas Marsden, Sloan, and Gleason considered the fate of Protestant and Catholic colleges and universities separately, James Burtchaell, C.S.C., considered the fate of both sets of Christian institutions. In *The Dying of the Light: The Disengagement of the Colleges and Universities from their Christian Churches,* Burtchaell explored how varying forms of secularization occurred at seventeen different colleges and universities that represented not only Protestant denominations but also Catholic religious orders. His narratives produce a common set of lessons. Perhaps the most significant lesson is that each of these institutions, at some point or another, made critical turns in terms of the sources from which they derived their identity. First, the church no longer became the institution from which religious colleges and universities derived their identity. Instead, identity came in relation to the larger culture in the United States. If the first turn was from the church to the state, the second turn was from the state to the academic guild. According to Burtchaell, "The greatest outside authority to which all of these colleges in our study now defer is that of the academy itself" (1998, p. 834). Once removed from "the support of the church or a denomination that had retained a sense of prophetic independence, the colleges were the more easily suborned by nationalism and its half brother, the jingoism of the academy" (Burtchaell, 1998, p. 834).

Although Burtchaell tends to see institutional secularization from a particular religious body as a key element in the resultant secularization of scholarship, in *The Sacred and Secular University,* Jon Roberts and James Turner (2000) provide a different historical analysis of the causes. They contend that the transformation of colleges into universities and the separation of the institutions from religious communities that formed them were only secondary factors. Instead they propose that the elevation of the arts and sciences in the new universities played a vital role in the secularization of scholarship. In particular, two key academic trends in the arts and sciences nurtured the secularization of scholarship: philological historicism in the humanities and methodological naturalism in the sciences.

For Roberts and Turner, philological historicism refers to the belief that "every human phenomenon was determined by its own distinct, unique, and ultimately contingent history" (2000, p. 118). Ultimately, they claim, "historicism eventually had the effect of sapping Christianity, indeed undermining any conviction of objective truth transcending human beings" (2000, p. 119). They define methodological or scientific naturalism as the trend to no longer accept a supernatural agency as a principle of explanation in science. Darwin's theory of origins provided the crucial proposal that "triggered the establishment of 'methodological naturalism' as the norm of scientific discourse" (2000, p. 28). The triumph of scientific naturalism was not sudden. Nonetheless, increasingly for scientists after Darwin, "The appropriate response to the inability to account for natural phenomena naturalistically was to solicit further scientific inquiry, not posit the supernatural" (2000, p. 29). The practical result for scientists was that "their work in the classroom and laboratory became theologically neutral—compatible with theism and atheism alike" (2000, p. 31). Eventually this "scientific method" was extended to the human sciences, with the similar result that theological or supernatural explanations were similarly avoided.

Despite the disagreement among historians about the causes and relationships between various forms of secularization, they all make one thing clear. The works of these historians provide numerous concrete historical examples of how the process of secularization in all its forms took hold in both Protestant and Catholic colleges and universities in the United States. As Rodney Sawatsky (2004) notes, "This metamorphosis of higher education can be seen as one of the clearest examples of secularization in American history" (p. 5).

Moreover, while historians argue about the importance of various factors regarding the secularization of scholarship, agreement exists about what factors to include. The majority of them acknowledge the role of:

The increasing belief that scientific naturalism was the primary means of determining the veracity of a particular truth claim. By their very nature, claims concerning theology and religious practices in relation to God are deemed generally implausible to affirm.

The development of historicism in the humanities, which served to undermine transcendent truth claims.

The process of accommodation initiated by religious leaders in an effort to try to make their claims concerning theology and religious practices plausible in light of scientific naturalism and historicism. This process was also accelerated, however, by key intellectuals in the United States, who sought to remove even such references from public discourse.

If claims about theology and religious practices were to persist outside theology departments, these claims were only acceptable as part of an individual's private life versus his or her public life. Claims in the arena of one's public life were deemed to be true in light of the means of scientific naturalism or were understood to be merely products of one's own historical situation.

Although historians have only recently helped describe both secularization as a whole and the secularization of scholarship in particular, from the very origins of their discipline sociologists began raising the deeper theoretical question about the phenomena of secularization. They propounded a theory of secularization that sought to make sense of the phenomena that historians described.

Is the Secularization of Higher Education Inevitable?

Is the secularization of religious colleges and universities inevitable? Only a few of the above historians offer answers to this question (see Dovre, 2002; Sterk, 2002). Some sociologists have, however, propounded a theory that elevated secularization from merely a word describing something that occurred in history to a social scientific theory that provides predictive power about the future of religion in society and religious higher education.

The secularization thesis might be said to be more of a metanarrative. David Martin describes this standard secularization narrative as beginning,

"Once there was *a* religious past, [which] has bit by bit emerged as *the* secular future. . . . The natural (often equated with science) wins out over religion through uninterrupted increments [however,] much religion resists and engages in rearguard actions" (2005, p. 8). Many early sociologists not only defended the standard narrative of secularization but also believed it could be used to claim predictive power about the future of religion. For instance, Auguste Comte claimed that modernization would lead society to evolve beyond the "theological stage." Frederich Engels thought the socialist revolution would lead to religion's demise, and Max Weber believed modernization would cause the "disenchantment" of the world (Stark, 1999). In the 1960s, Peter Berger predicted that religious believers would "be found only in small sects, huddled together to resist a worldwide secular culture" (1968, p. 3). By the early 1970s, William Swatos and Kevin Christiano (2000) tell us, "Secularization was the reigning dogma in the field" (p. 2). Whether or not this secularization story ends happily depends on one's ideological commitments. On one hand, some may see secularization as the emancipation of humanity from religious oppression. On the other hand, some may see secularization as the tragic reduction of the influence of Christianity in the West (see Marsden and Longfield, 1992, pp. 5–7).

Events in higher education broadly and scholarship in particular appeared to confirm this theory. In *The Academic Revolution,* Christopher Jencks and David Riesman went so far as to question the very future of church-related higher education in the United States (2002). Even Burtchaell described this secularization process as "inexorable" (1994, p. 132). Higher education, it appeared, provided the empirical evidence confirming the secularization thesis at all levels of the definition.

Deconstructing the Secularization Narrative

A number of scholars have begun deconstructing the secularization metanarrative. Sociologists beginning with David Martin (1965) and later Peter Berger himself voiced extensive disagreement about secularization and its characteristics. An important part of the debate has involved what exactly secularization theory entails (see essays on the debate in "After Secularization,"

2006). If secularization refers merely to the first or second type of secularization, what Stark calls "a decline in the social power of once dominant religious institutions whereby other social institutions, especially political and educational institutions, have escaped from prior religious domination," there is little debate that such secularization occurred in Europe and portions of North America (1999, p. 253). Certainly in higher education governance, funding, ethos, and curriculum, a good case for secularization can be made. Nonetheless, sociologists have questioned whether secularization is more of a regional phenomenon than the inevitable result that will occur around the world as modernization increases (see Sommerville, 2006; Schultz, 2006; Asad, 2003; Swatos and Olson, 2000). For instance, the Islamic resurgence in Iran, Turkey, and Afghanistan and the re-Christianization of Eastern Europe and a large portion of the republics that were once part of the Soviet Union would appear to undermine the theory.

The other three understandings, however, are what are usually referred to in the sociological discussion of what is called "secularization theory." As William Swatos and Daniel Olson note, "The principal thrust in secularization theory has . . . , been stronger than simply church-state issues or the scope of religious authority. It has been a claim that, in the face of scientific rationality, religion's influence on all aspects of life—from personal habits—to social institutions—is in dramatic decline" (2000, p. 6). Likewise, José Casanova (1994) asserts that secularization involves not only institutional differentiation but also the privatization of religion and religious outlooks.

It is this broad claim about religion's demise that has received more extensive critique. In *The Secular Revolution: Power, Interests and Conflict in the Secularization of American Public Life,* Christian Smith (2003) offers a comprehensive analysis of what is wrong with the theory: "Traditional secularization theory suffers from (1) far too much abstraction; (2) a lack of human agency; (3) a sense of over-deterministic inevitability; (4) an orientation (primarily among historians) of idealist intellectual history; (5) an over-romanticization of the religious past; (6) an overemphasis on religious self-destruction; and (7) an under-specification of the causal mechanisms of secularization" (p. 14). Smith's critique is especially important when considering the secularization of higher education and the questions we quoted from George Marsden at the beginning of this chapter. As Smith notes, early sociologists (and, we would add, some historians) located the causes of secularization more in impersonal movements such as modernization, science, industrialization, and historicism or in the religious groups themselves. In contrast Smith argues "that American public life was secularized by groups of rising scientific, academic, and literary intellectuals whose upward mobility—made possible by expanding industrial capitalism and an enlarging state—was obstructed by the Protestant establishment" (2003, p. 37). Smith also notes that assigning causal power to impersonal forces such as modernization and science diminishes these relational and institutional contexts. Secularization, according to Smith, was not neutral or impersonal in nature "but a reconstructed moral order [that] would increase their own group status, autonomy, authority, and eventually income" (2003, p. 37). Hugh McLeod, in his *Secularisation in Western Europe, 1848–1914,* agrees with Smith. Secularization, McLeod claims, is not "an impersonal 'process'" and that "it would be better to see it [the process] as a 'contest,' in which adherents of rival worldviews battled it out" (2000, p. 28).

If secularization is not an inevitable "impersonal process," a sort of predetermined end of the march of history, but is instead merely the result of what might be considered a tournament of worldviews or narratives, then there is no reason to believe that the secularization of higher education or scholarship is inevitable. According to this alternative account, it is too soon to say religiously informed views cannot play a vital role in the academic conversation. In fact, the secularization theory may be considered the legitimating narrative told by one particular group that won the most recent battles and wish to see the battle ended. If at some points secularization and secularization theory are a result of a power struggle between worldviews or overarching narratives (that is, metanarratives) with particular philosophies of history, however, then the enforcement or encouragement of secularization may not always involve the triumph of universal reason but may at times involve the repression of other ways of knowing. Perhaps secular forms and understandings of reason are merely one among many competing schools of thought in the tournament of historical and academic narratives.

In the introduction to a volume simply titled *Radical Orthodoxy*, we find an example of scholars who are beginning to develop this line of argument. The authors, John Milbank, Graham Ward, and Catherine Pickstock, contend that secularism is not only a competing worldview or narrative but also increasingly problematic: "For several centuries now, secularism has been defining and constructing the world. It is a world in which the theological is either discredited or turned into a harmless leisure-time activity of private commitment. . . . Today the logic of secularism is imploding. Speaking with a microphoned and digitally stimulated voice, it proclaims—uneasily, or else increasingly unashamedly—its own lack of values and lack of meaning. In its cyberspaces and theme parks it promotes a materialism [that] is soulless, aggressive, nonchalant and nihilistic" (1999, p. 1).

In contrast to the secularization of scholarship, these advocates of what they also call "radical orthodoxy" suggest a different way: "The central theological framework of radical orthodoxy is 'participation' as developed by Plato and reworked by Christianity, because any alternative configuration perforce reserves a territory independent of God" (1999, p. 3). As a result "worship or doxology is not confined to a religious compartment of human existence but rather spills over into every sphere of human activity, from agriculture to commerce, from recreation to parenting" (Smith, 2004, p. 170). For these scholars the plausibility of God is defined by God's ability through practices such as the sacraments to shape and reshape the identity of people and thus how scholars view the world and their work.

In light of this assumption, radical orthodoxy seeks to employ critical tools of postmodernity such as deconstruction (as initiated by Jacques Derrida) and archaeology (as initiated by Michel Foucault) in an attempt to clear the space necessary for theology to once again assert a place not only in the academy but also in society as a whole. The aspiration of these scholars is not only to expose the assumptions inherent in the current secular structure of scholarship in the academy but also in many ways to replace it for Christians with structures predicated on one's participatory experience with God. *Radical Orthodoxy* (1999) includes chapters seeking to establish this kind of work in fields such as language, aesthetics, and music. Other volumes produced by authors identified with radical orthodoxy also seek to "overcome the [accommodating] pathos of modern theology, and to restore in postmodern terms, the possibility of theology as a metadiscourse" (Milbank, 1991, p. 1; see also Long, 2000; Ward, 2000).

The radical dimension initiated by such efforts as radical orthodoxy is not so much vested in attempts to reestablish theology as a discourse that can reach across all other forms of academic discourse in attempts to initiate the postsecular. In his book *Introducing Radical Orthodoxy*, James K. A. Smith contends that this movement offers a "more consistent postmodernism, one that follows through on the internal deconstruction of the Enlightenment project rather than halting it at the point of liberal politics and the classical critique of religion. The church, authentically conceived, should be the quintessential site of such a post-secular engagement" (2004, p. 61). Such a move on the part of the radical orthodoxy movement also counters the trajectory detailed by Howard and Burtchaell in terms of where the academy derives its identity. Instead of the state or the professional guilds, scholars in the academy may once again be able to derive their identity from the church. In relation to scholarship, such an identity collapses a host of myths perpetuated by the Enlightenment. In the end, rejecting the "myth of secularity allows theology in mainstream discourse to be unapologetically confessional and Christian research across the disciplines to be unapologetically theological" (Smith, 2004, p. 74).

As the following chapters demonstrate, radical orthodoxy is merely one group of scholars among many seeking, in some sense, to challenge the secularization of scholarship. In this respect, the turn of the twenty-first century brought with it very different ramifications than the turn of the twentieth century in terms of the ability of religious faith to inform the nature of scholarship. Although the theory of secularization may not be completely dead, its inevitability is certainly questioned and challenged in the academy. The academy may lack the sense of consensus it once had concerning the ability of religious faith to inform the nature of scholarship, but the hold that modernity established at the turn of the twentieth century had certainly declined by the turn of the twenty-first century. The next chapter identifies and describes ways that three religious traditions nurtured faith-informed understandings of reason and scholarship that contrast with some of the dominant understandings in the academy.

Faith-Informed Traditions of Practical Rationality: Contemporary Approaches of Three Religious Traditions to Knowledge

L ITTLE CONTROVERSY EXISTS about the diversity of higher education institutions available. We expect and even honor the fact that the ethos and culture of different schools will be distinctive, depending on the various identity labels of the institution. With regard to religious institutions, observers recognize that the mission and ethos of Catholic, Lutheran, Evangelical, Jewish, Baptist, or Mennonite institutions are different (see, for example, Edwards, 2006; Riley, 2005; Benne, 2001).

When it comes to scholarship, this recognition or celebration of the influence of religious diversity is much different. After George Marsden (1994) ended his chronicle of the secularization of American higher education in *The Soul of the American University*, he concluded with a provocative postscript about the future direction of religion and higher education. The secularization of the academy had gone too far, he claimed. He went on to argue "there is no reason why it should be a rule of academia that *no* religious viewpoint shall receive serious consideration" (p. 431). Moreover, he suggested that the academy should perhaps even encourage scholarship from the perspective of particular religious traditions.

In a review of Marsden's book, Bruce Kuklick (1996) took particular exception to Marsden's proposal:

"Does he think that at his university, Notre Dame, they teach a Roman Catholic chemistry? . . . Would Calvin College actually devote itself to a Presbyterian anthropology or worry that Episcopal psychology should get a hearing? Should historians of the Reformation be primarily identified as Protestant, French or female?" (p. 82).

Kuklick's worry about religiously based identity scholarship echoes a common modern concern about identity-based scholarship, whether it is associated with gender, ethnicity, race, or religion. This view holds that the standards and methods associated with one's professional identity (historian, biologist, psychologist, for example) and the knowledge one acquires through applying those standards and methods should not be influenced by one's other particular identities (woman, Southerner, Democrat, Baptist, German ethnicity, for example). To be a professional scholar means that one attempts to study nature, society, history, and more by removing oneself from the influence of these identities and the narratives, beliefs, practices, and traditions associated with them (except of course one's professional identity). Kuklick, in other words, argues for maintaining the two-spheres approach to professional scholarship and knowledge that Sloan argues many nonreligious scholars and mainline Protestants have long adopted.

In contrast to Kuklick, we contend that by understanding and being sensitive to the different approaches to scholarship supported and encouraged by different religious traditions, one can better understand the contemporary debate about religion and scholarship in American higher education. Only then can one fully appreciate and understand the positive possibility of scholarship informed by a religious tradition. To advance this argument, we recount the religious sources of a countercultural trend in the academy. Before postmodernism became fashionable, the Catholic, Anabaptist, and Reformed religious traditions nurtured alternatives to the modern concept of tradition-free reasoning by supporting epistemological methods and outlooks friendly to "tradition-based thinking." As a result, they also helped foster contemporary scholars who are now major contributors to the debate about religion and scholarship in the postmodern academy and the relationship of religious traditions to academic theorizing and reasoning.

The Roman Catholic Tradition

The Catholic tradition of faith-informed scholarship exemplified by church fathers such as Augustine precedes the invention of the university. In addition, as mentioned in the previous chapter, the history of universities and thinking about them includes such prominent Catholic thinkers as Thomas Aquinas and John Henry Newman. We will not attempt to summarize the complex and diverse approaches to faith and knowledge fostered over these years by various Catholic thinkers, but we want to highlight important differences between the Catholic approach to scholarship and the general mainline Protestant approach.

Despite their ancient and esteemed history, Catholics were initially considered outsiders to an American education system dominated by mainline Protestants (Carpenter, 2002; Gleason, 1995). The tension that persisted up until recently between Catholics and Protestants in the United States often kept scholars in their respective colleges and universities in separate and distinct cultural spheres. In particular, mainline Protestants viewed their Catholic counterparts as being tied to the church's dogma and its authoritarian hierarchy. Although outsiders to the dominant mainline Protestant college ethos in America, Catholic institutions and intellectuals through their connections to the larger international Catholic tradition were able to develop a robust countercultural response to modernity after World War I. The Scholastic Revival, as it became known, developed a revised version of Thomas Aquinas's thought, Neo-Thomism, to help guide it. Neo-Thomism gave Catholics a comprehensive philosophy of life that included a distinctive vision for art, economics, psychology, ethics, and history. Some Catholics even described it as a Catholic *Weltanschauung* or worldview that could serve as the basis for a Catholic culture (Gleason, 1995, p. 115). Although the movement varied, as Gleason (1995) notes, "The view that prevailed among most Catholics, however, was that Neoscholastic philosophy was authentically philosophical because its truths were arrived at by a process of autonomous reasoning. The outcome of philosophical reasoning agreed with revelation because God was the author of truth in both realms" (p. 116). In other words, this vision was based on the idea that reason was coherent with and supported faith. According to Gleason, the vision resulted in three key characteristics of the Catholic worldview at that time. First, it purported to claim that God's existence could be proved by reason alone. Second, it emphasized "the mind's capacity to arrive at objective truth through the direct intuitions of the intellect and the exercise of discursive reason" (p. 118). Third, this system provided

Catholics with an all-encompassing philosophy of life that could be applied to every discipline.

Despite this powerful counter to the two-sphere approach of mainline Protestants, events in the 1950s and 1960s such as resurgent anti-Catholicism, sharper discipline from the Vatican, the vast exodus from Catholic priesthood and various orders, and the resistance of younger faculty to neo-Thomism created a crisis in Catholic colleges and universities with regard to modernity. Gleason writes, "What happened in the 1960s climaxed the transition from an era in which Catholic educators challenged modernity to one in which they accepted modernity" (1995, p. 318). Unlike many mainline Protestant schools that secularized to accommodate modern scientific approaches to knowledge, however, most Catholic schools retained a strong sense of Catholic identity. The problem was that they no longer shared a common understanding of what it meant to be Catholic. This "identity crisis" involved: "a lack of consensus as to the substantive content of the ensemble of religious beliefs, moral commitments, and academic assumptions that supposedly constitute Catholic identity, and a consequent inability to specify what that identity entails for the practical functioning of Catholic colleges and universities. . . . They are no longer sure what remaining Catholic means" (Gleason, 1995, p. 320). This identity crisis was compounded by the sudden shortage of men and women joining religious orders and thus providing leadership for Catholic colleges and universities. Without the efforts of these individuals, Catholic colleges and universities were forced to obtain the services of laypeople, many of whom were not as well trained in the teachings of the church (Morey and Piderit, 2006).

Pope John Paul II's 1990 encyclical *On Catholic Universities: Ex Corde Ecclesiae* (1990) sought to address this crisis in Catholic universities as a whole. It also remains an important contemporary summary of the official Catholic approach to issues regarding faith and knowledge. In the first part of the document, Pope John Paul II set forth the ways "Catholic ideals, attitudes and principles penetrate and inform university activities in accordance with the proper nature and autonomy of these activities" (*Ex Corde*, Part I, A, 1, section 14). Particularly with regard to the scholarship of research or discovery, *Ex Corde* identified four important aspects where the Catholic tradition and research meet: "*(a)* the search for an *integration of knowledge, (b)* a *dialogue between faith and reason, (c)* an *ethical concern,* and *(d)* a *theological perspective*" (section 15).

"The search for an integration of knowledge," according to *Ex Corde,* means that Catholic universities and scholars will not be content with the fragmentation of knowledge in the contemporary university but that they will instead work toward "a higher synthesis of knowledge, in which alone lies the possibility of satisfying that thirst for truth [that] is profoundly inscribed on the heart of the human person" (section 16). One finds this theme represented in Catholic scholars such as Mark Roche (2003), who argues that "collaborative work across the disciplines is a moral imperative," (p. 36) and Alasdair MacIntyre's claim (2006) that the special task of the American Catholic university "should be to challenge its secular counterparts by recovering both for them and for itself a less fragmented conception of what an education beyond high school should be . . ." (p. 10). According *to Ex Corde,* this statement means that "university scholars will be engaged in a constant effort to determine the relative place and meaning of each of the various disciplines within the context of a vision of the human person and the world that is enlightened by the Gospel, and therefore by a faith in Christ, the *Logos,* as the centre of creation and of human history" (section 16).

In this respect, *Ex Corde* reiterates the suggestion made by John Henry Newman that "*Theology* plays a particularly important role in the search for a synthesis of knowledge as well as in the dialogue between faith and reason" (section 19). As the queen of the sciences, "it serves all other disciplines in their search for meaning, not only by helping them to investigate how their discoveries will affect individuals and society but also by bringing a perspective and an orientation not contained within their own methodologies" (section 19). *Ex Corde* admits, however, that the dialogue is two way: "In turn, interaction with these other disciplines and their discoveries enriches theology, offering it a better understanding of the world today, and making theological research more relevant to current needs" (section 19). Catholic thinkers have echoed this pronouncement by questioning why theology is excluded from the curricular requirements of universities (O'Brien, 2002).

The dialogue between faith and reason is needed, according to *Ex Corde*, "so that it can be seen more profoundly how faith and reason bear harmonious witness to the unity of all truth" (section 17). Although *Ex Corde* acknowledges that various disciplines use different methods of inquiry, it also contends such research "can never truly conflict with faith" because "the things of the earth and the concerns of faith derive from the same God" (section 17). *Ex Corde* thus affirms a Catholic belief, demonstrated in thinkers such as Thomas Aquinas, that truths of faith and reason can be synthesized together into a larger coherent whole.

Ex Corde also echoes a common refrain among religious scholars that what religion offers is a moral framework for scholarship. It states, "Because knowledge is meant to serve the human person, research in a Catholic University is always carried out with a concern for the *ethical* and *moral implications* both of its methods and of its discoveries" (section 18). It cites science and technology as two major areas where such concern is needed and concludes, "Men and women of science will truly aid humanity only if they preserve 'the sense of the transcendence of the human person over the world and of God over the human person'" (section 18).

The insistence on the unity of truth or knowledge and the harmonious witness of faith and reason are central themes of the Catholic tradition that stand in stark contrast to the two-spheres approach of mainline Protestantism. The Jacobsens (2004) claim that this emphasis also leads to a uniquely Catholic emphasis on interdisciplinary work and the overall need for communities and institutions to sustain scholarly work (p. 81). Since its release, the community of Catholic scholars have expanded on *Ex Corde*'s vision in various ways, and as a result a vigorous conversation is occurring among various Catholic scholars about what both Catholic higher education and Catholic scholarship entail or what the Catholic intellectual tradition is (see Morey and Piderit, 2006; Roche, 2003; O'Brien, 2002; Wilcox and King, 2000; Buckley, 1998).

For institutions, questions persist about whether this distinctively Catholic approach to faith and knowledge will continue to be transmitted by Catholic institutions or whether they may follow the path of mainline Protestantism toward a two-spheres model that accommodates by fragmentation and secularization. This concern is reinforced by the title and content of Melanie M. Morey and John J. Piderit's *Catholic Higher Education: A Culture in Crisis* (2006), a recent study of thirty-three Catholic colleges and universities. Morey and Piderit conclude, "A Catholic cultural crisis is looming within American Catholic higher education" (p. 347). The reason is that they found two things in their field research: "First, Catholic components as they now exist at most Catholic colleges are so understated or subtle they can be easily overlooked or ignored. Second, administrators know little about the Catholic tradition they so enthusiastically champion" (p. 347).

We would suggest that perhaps one reason for the former point is the traditional Catholic focus on the unity of truth as well as the harmonious witness of reason and faith. This emphasis leads to less emphasis on the distinctive contributions of a particular Christian tradition to knowledge or a particular scholar's Christian commitment to scholarship. Because some Catholic scholars would argue that they see the truths of reason they discover as the same as the truths of faith, they do not spend time explicitly pointing out how their scholarly work draws on the teachings of the Church. One important exception, however, is a prominent philosopher who is rearticulating a traditional Catholic vision that also highlights the importance and need for understanding the influence of diverse traditions on reasoning.

One major question for Catholic thinkers with a high confidence in human reason is to explain the failure of reason to help us achieve unified systems of thought and answers to perplexing questions. Alasdair MacIntyre, whom Roche (2003) calls "one of the world's leading Catholic philosophers" (p. 47) has provided one of the most powerful answers to that question. MacIntyre takes an explicitly Catholic (he labels it Thomistic) approach to ethics and philosophy (see, for example, Morey and Piderit, 2006, pp. 119–120). Before he identified himself as a Thomist, MacIntyre sought in his book, *After Virtue* (1984), to defend and reformulate what he called the tradition of the virtues. An important part of MacIntyre's argument and where he differs somewhat from the earlier Catholic Neoscholastics is his contention that there is no such thing as universal rationality divorced from a particular tradition. Thus, to be part of a community in which one can acquire the intellectual and moral virtues, one must affiliate with a community that represents a particular tradition. He concludes that to sustain the virtues, we will have to turn to communities "in which civility and the intellectual and moral life can be sustained through the new dark ages which are already upon us" (p. 263).

In *Whose Justice? Which Rationality?* MacIntyre (1988) defends his view that concepts of both justice and rationality depend on a particular tradition. He argues that the Enlightenment provided an ideal of rational justification but that this ideal has proved impossible to attain. Moreover, the Enlightenment blinded us to what we need to recover: "a conception of rational enquiry, as embodied in a tradition, a conception according to which the standards of rational justification themselves emerge from and are part of a history in which they are vindicated by the way in which they transcended the limitations of and provide remedies for the defects of their predecessors within the history of that same tradition" (p. 7). MacIntyre notes that it is important to understand four things about tradition-embedded rational inquiry. First, it is historical. In other words, "to justify is to narrate how the argument has gone so far" (1988, p. 8). Second, "doctrines, theses, and arguments all have to be understood in terms of historical context." Third, because rationality comes in multiple forms, the resolution of differences between traditions requires understanding this reality. Fourth, "the concept of tradition-constituted and tradition-constitutive rational enquiry cannot be elucidated apart from its exemplifications . . . " (1988, p. 10). This argument, as MacIntyre demonstrates using Augustine and Thomas Aquinas, has clear implications for the relationship among religion, scholars, and scholarship. MacIntyre also clearly states that he himself identifies with the Thomistic strand of Augustinian Christianity. Later in the *Three Rival Versions of Moral Enquiry,* MacIntyre (1990) defends this tradition against what he calls the encyclopedic tradition and the genealogical tradition. Again, the test for these traditions is how well they are lived and passed along in communities and how well they handle new challenges.

Much of this book and this chapter could be said to offer support for MacIntyre's argument. In contrast to an Enlightenment model of knowledge, the one basically adopted by mainline Protestants, other religious traditions offer approaches to practical rationality and knowledge that narrate a different story about reality and the university. These rival versions of inquiry are represented by scholars and embodied in religious universities in a way that they set forth an alternative vision of scholarship. In particular, two traditions somewhat associated with Evangelical Christianity have attempted to set forth their own visions.

The Reformed Worldview

Traditionally, institutions and scholars affiliated with the Reformed tradition were heavily influenced by the Reformation thought of John Calvin. Joel Carpenter (2002) writes of scholars and universities in this tradition:

> *They ascribe to God the greatest glory and majesty imaginable, seeing the Almighty One as the great creator and governor of the universe. . . . The Reformed see the world also as the arena for the Biblical drama of salvation, whereby God's good and perfect universe, which has been marred and besieged by sin, is being redeemed. To save the world, God became human in Jesus of Nazareth, to free humanity from bondage to sin and ultimately to restore creation to its unblemished glory. For the Reformed, then, God's plan of salvation goes far beyond the personal rescue of human souls; it involves society, nature, and indeed the entire cosmos. Jesus is both the messiah of oppressed humanity and cosmic lord and savior of the universe [pp. 186–187].*

Although churches in the Reformed tradition accounted for a third of the pre–Civil War colleges in America (including schools such as Princeton), many of them eventually followed the intellectual patterns of mainline Protestantism as a whole and adopted the two-realm approach to knowledge (Burtchaell, 1998; Sloan, 1994; Marsden, 1994). As a result, vestiges of Calvinist thought influence few of these institutions today (Carpenter, 2002). Nonetheless, a small group of Reformed schools and scholars inspired by the influential Dutch theologian, politician, philosopher, and founder of the Free University Amsterdam, Abraham Kuyper (1837–1920), have helped sustain a different approach to understanding the relationship between faith and learning that has made substantial contributions to evangelical Protestantism, the larger Christian world, and the secular academy (Turner, 2003; Wolfe, 2000).

Kuyper, like many Christians, interpreted the intellectual secularization he encountered in Europe not as the result of the benign influence of modernization and pluralism but as an expression of humanity's rebellion against God. Kuyper, however, proposed a new response that differed from mainline scholars, Catholics, and evangelicals. Mainline scholars largely answered intellectual secularization by using their two-realm theory of truth. Catholics adopted a form of Neo-Scholasticism with a high confidence in reason. Many evangelicals retreated into isolation where they attempted to return to old patterns of Christian thought and life. In contrast, Kuyper articulated ways Christians and the church could and should embrace pluralism while also emphasizing "the value-laden, commitment-driven nature of knowledge" (Carpenter, 2002, p. 189).

Kuyper accomplished both these goals by developing two key concepts. First, in the public life of a nation, Kuyper embraced what has come to be called "principled pluralism" (Skillen and McCarthy, 1991). Kuyper claimed that in a fallen world people would join together in groups that "shared a singular view of reality, a distinctive pattern for living, and a sociopolitical agenda" (Carpenter, 2002, p. 189). A just state would not favor one particular group by establishing a Christian or secularist state but would recognize this plurality of institutions and interests. In other words, it would seek to ensure justice is undertaken toward each group (and not merely individuals) and each institutional sphere (family, church, education, art, for example) in which it participated. It should be noted that Kuyper did not believe the church as an institution should guide and direct each sphere. In light of the discussion of secularization in the previous chapter, Skillen and McCarthy's important distinction (1991) is helpful:

> On the one hand, Kuyper, along with many Catholics and other Protestants, [was] a vigorous opponent of secularization, if by "secularization" is meant the outworking of the spirit of liberalism and revolution [that] claims that humans have no master in history and no ordinances from God to bind them—the claim that human beings are autonomous in their freedom to shape politics, art, science, education and all of culture. Yet, unlike most Catholics and many Protestants of his day, Kuyper [was] a strong promoter of the

secularization process[,] if by "secularization" is meant the libera-
tion of different social "spheres" from ecclesiastical control [p. 241].

Kuyper's second intellectual development involved challenging the fact-value distinction promoted by modern thinkers such as Max Weber. Instead of accepting this distinction, Kuyper emphasized the value-laden, commitment-driven nature of all knowledge. To communicate this concept, he emphasized the importance of a person's worldview (Naugle, 2002). Kuyper described this idea in his famous Stone Lectures at Princeton University in 1898:

> *As truly as every plant has a root, so truly does a principle hide*
> *under every manifestation of life. These principles are intercon-*
> *nected, and have their common root in a fundamental principle;*
> *and from the latter is developed logically and systematically the*
> *whole complex of ruling ideas and conceptions that go to make up*
> *our life and world-view. With such a coherent world and life-view,*
> *firmly resting on its principle and self consistent in its splendid*
> *structure, Modernism now confronts Christianity; and against this*
> *deadly danger, Christians cannot successfully defend [our] sanctu-*
> *ary, but by placing in opposition to all this, a life- and world-view*
> *of [our] own, founded as firmly on the base of [our] own principle,*
> *wrought out with the same clearness and glittering in an equally*
> *logical consistency [1994, pp. 189–190].*

After the Stone Lectures, Kuyper visited various Reformed communities in the upper Midwest such as Calvin College, where his thinking would have a lasting impact on the intellectual climate (Carpenter, 2002; Benne, 2001).

Carpenter, the former provost at Calvin College, summarizes the Kuyperian perspective that has emerged today from Kuyper's intellectual descendents: "Kuyperians do not believe that reason or rationality alone drives such investigations, nor that these modes of thought determine the context from which our thinking emanates. Differences between scholars very often go all the way back to differing worldviews, divergent basic assumptions, and opposing religious beliefs. Even work in the natural sciences is socially situated and conditioned by the predispositions that the scientist brings to the bench" (2002, p. 191). Based on this approach, thinkers influenced by the Reformed Kuyperian tradition such as George Marsden, Nicholas Wolterstorff, and Alvin Plantinga have made the case that "scholars who have religious faith should be reflecting on the intellectual implications of that faith and bringing those reflections into the mainstream of intellectual life" (Marsden, 1997, pp. 3–4).

One concrete way that these Reformed scholars have attempted to undertake this approach is in the field of analytical philosophy. Ironically, perhaps one of the most direct assaults on the plausibility of God from the analytical side was offered in a collection of essays authored by Bertrand Russell. In *Why I Am Not a Christian,* Russell begins by laying out the various propositions that Christianity has often referenced in relation to the existence of God. Such propositions include the argument from design, the argument from first-cause, and the argument from natural law. Russell goes on to contend that these arguments all prove to be implausible. In their place, he subsequently asserts that "the Christian God may exist; so may the Gods of Olympus, or of ancient Egypt, or of Babylon. But no one of these hypotheses is more probable than any other: they lie outside the region of even probable knowledge, and therefore there is no reason to consider any of them" (1957, p. 51).

Although cast in the same methodological mold as Bertrand Russell, Reformed analytical philosophers such as Nicholas Wolterstorff (1999) and Alvin Plantinga (2000) have developed quite different views concerning the plausibility of God and subsequently the role that belief in God would play in relation to scholarship. They have challenged the very methodological commitments that came to define analytical philosophy and have claimed that just as contentions concerning the implausibility of belief in God had foreclosed possibilities for religious faith to play a role in scholarship, contentions concerning the plausibility of belief in God would reopen possibilities for religious faith to play a role in scholarship.

To accomplish this task these philosophers have sought to reconfigure the relationship between faith and reason. For example, in 1976 Nicholas Wolterstorff published a small book entitled *Reason Within the Bounds of Religion,* which was an obvious play off Immanual Kant's *Religion Within the Bounds of Reason.* In the book, Wolterstorff made a philosophical argument defending the Kuyperian outlook with regard to academic theorizing. He argued that when making theories, scholars work with three kinds of beliefs: data beliefs, data-background beliefs, and control beliefs. Data beliefs are basic testable assertions about reality. For example, if our theory is "Santa Claus does not live at the North Pole," data beliefs would include our basic understanding of the definition of the North Pole and how to find it. Data-background beliefs include what a scholar is willing to accept as evidence (for example, photographs of the North Pole). Control beliefs, however, are those beliefs that determine what counts as an acceptable theory. They "include beliefs about the requisite logical or aesthetic structure of a theory, beliefs about the entities to whose existence a theory may correctly commit us and the like" (1999, pp. 67–68). For example, the control belief in this theory might be that "theories postulating nonsensory entities are unsatisfactory" (1999, p. 68).

Control beliefs, Wolterstorff argued, serve as the basis for reasoning and evaluating knowledge and academic theories. It is true for every practitioner in the academy, whether religious or secular. At that time most scholars accepted the idea that everyone made decisions about data beliefs and data-background beliefs. But Wolterstorff argued that all scholars, including secular scholars, had control beliefs that shaped their theories in unique ways. In light of this point, Wolterstorff concluded that "it is not the case that one is warranted in accepting some theory if and only if one is warranted in believing that it is justified by propositions knowable noninferentially and with certitude" (1999, pp. 56–57). In fact, warranted belief can and often does come in inferential terms. In *Warranted Christian Belief,* Alvin Plantinga (2000) expanded this line of thought by establishing an understanding of Christian belief deemed to have warrant.

Efforts by Reformed scholars such as Wolterstorff, Plantinga, and Marsden have advanced the Kuyperian idea that all scholarship proceeds from a worldview and that Christians must undertake their scholarly work with this worldview in mind. After all, a scholar's beliefs will subsequently have bearing on the theories or conceptual frameworks he or she may use in relation to his or her pursuit of truth. As Alvin Plantinga (1994) argued, "If we take for granted a Christian explanatory background, we might come up with an entirely different view. What we need here is scholarship that takes account of all that we know and thus takes account of what we know as Christians" (p. 292).

This Reformed or Kuyperian perspective about the importance of one's worldview for theorizing has played an important role among the evangelical Protestants and the evangelical Christian college community, including the more than one hundred colleges and universities associated with the Council for Christian Colleges and Universities (discussed more fully later). Despite Mark Noll's critique of evangelical Christianity's sparse contribution to academia in *The Scandal of the Evangelical Mind*, he notes at the end of his book that an evangelical renaissance may be under way, partly through the influence of the Reformed tradition.

In contrast to a two-realm theory of faith and learning and similar to the MacIntyrian approach that emphasizes the importance of tradition-formed reason, Reformed thinkers have influenced these schools to develop teaching and produce scholarship concerned with the "integration of faith and learning" or acquiring a "Christian worldview" (Jacobsen and Jacobsen, 2004; Litfin, 2004; Benne, 2001; Marsden, 1997). Arthur Holmes, a former philosophy professor at Wheaton College and a proponent of the Reformed worldview language and approach, was one of the key figures in this movement through such books as *The Idea of a Christian College* (1975) and *All Truth Is God's Truth* (1977). Holmes argued that Christian scholars should examine and critique the fundamental assumptions of their disciplines in light of a Christian worldview. To help students with this task, Christian colleges should also require courses on developing a Christian worldview. Today, at many CCCU colleges, one can find general education courses that address the acquisition and application of a Christian worldview.

The Anabaptist Narrative

Although not as influential to date in the larger academy as the Reformed or Catholic traditions, the Anabaptists, according to Mark Noll, have also played an important role in revitalizing the conversation about faith and learning among Evangelical institutions and intellectuals. The distinctive Anabaptist outlook developed during the Reformation through the influence of various thinkers such as Menno Simons. Their unique way of living is manifest, especially in the church:

The church in Anabaptist-Mennonite thought is the body of Christ defined by the life and teaching of Jesus, transformed by the death and resurrection of Jesus the Christ and empowered by the Holy Spirit. As the primary vehicle through which God today works His will in the world, the church is to be separated from and nonconformed to the world, yet is also salt and light in the world and the agency of God's reconciling love in the world. The church, accordingly, is visible and tangible for it embraces all those who are baptized as adults upon confession of faith in Christ and who commit themselves to follow the way of Christ in fellowship [Sawatsky, 1997, p. 194].

The unique narrative and practices of the church, Anabaptists believe, also should influence how scholarship is approached.

Of various scholars, it has been the Anabaptist theologian John Howard Yoder, a former professor at the University of Notre Dame and Goshen College, who perhaps most effectively articulated the Anabaptist rationale for the unique practices and lifestyle that Anabaptists embody in their churches and institutions. Similar to what Kuyper did for Reformed thinking, Yoder articulated a number of important aspects of Anabaptist thought that challenged modern approaches to knowledge. First, he challenged the modern notion of ahistorical reason and in its place articulated the importance of Christ-formed reasoning and living. Second, he believed this reasoning and living must take place in the midst of the church, which seeks to embody obedience to Christ's teaching about the Kingdom of God. "The church precedes the world epistemologically. We know more fully from Jesus Christ and in the context of the confessed faith than we know in other ways. The meaning and validity and limits of concepts like 'nature' or of 'science' are best seen not when looked at alone but in light of the confession of the lordship of Christ. The church precedes the world as well axiologically, in that the Lordship of Christ is the center which must guide critical value choices, so that we may be called to subordinate or even to reject those values which contradict Jesus" (1984, p. 11). This focus on the church as the embodiment of Christ's teaching and God's work in the world and its importance for shaping faith-informed reasoning have had important implications for how Anabaptists approach higher education. The education of Anabaptists tends to place an importance on being a distinct community with a unique guiding purpose. As Rodney Sawatsky notes, Mennonite colleges are called on "to nurture citizens of God's kingdom rather than of the nation" (1997, p. 199). To use postmodern language, Anabaptists have often seen themselves as living, writing, and adhering to a different narrative than the narrative composed by the American academy. Not surprisingly, teaching Mennonite college students Mennonite history, especially the Anabaptist story, is a frequent means to reproduce a separated church.

As a result, contemporary Anabaptists in the postmodern world now see their adopted and lived narratives as also shaping their educational and scholarly practices. David Weaver-Zercher claims, "Anabaptists share an overlapping array of narratives, rituals and symbols that allow them to fashion their own form of Christian scholarship. And it should therefore not be surprising that the scholarship produced by Anabaptists has exhibited distinctive hues and trumpeted particular themes" (2004, p. 111). Weaver-Zercher makes his case by citing *The Missing Peace: The Search for Nonviolent Alternatives in United States History* by James Juhnke and Carol Hunter (2001). Juhnke and Hunter point out how many interpretations of U.S. history sanction violence and fail to consider the possibility of nonviolence. Weaver-Zercher's edited collection, *Minding the Church: Scholarship in the Anabaptist Tradition* (2002), provides additional stories from Anabaptist scholars about how they understand their narrative relating to scholarship.

Perhaps the most influential work outlining this approach is *Scholarship and Christian Faith: Enlarging the Conversation* (2004) by Douglas and Rhonda Jacobsen. The Jacobsens insist that Anabaptists differ from Reformed scholars because they want to emphasize the importance not only of one's worldview or narrative for distinctive scholarship but also the virtues developed in a community formed by that narrative or worldview. To illustrate their point, the Jacobsens cite the work of the Anabaptist scholar Nancey Murphy. Murphy has written extensively about the relationship between religion and science in works such as *Bodies and Souls, or Spirited Bodies?* (2006), *Reconciling Theology and Science: A Radical Reformation Perspective* (1997), and, with George Ellis, *On the Moral Nature of the Universe: Theology, Cosmology and Ethics* (1996). In contrast to modern views that see knowledge as "a large public building constructed on the solid foundation of incontestable, objective facts about the world" (Jacobsen and Jacobsen, 2004, p. 54), she views knowledge in a much more communal manner. According to the Jacobsens (2004), Murphy claims that "we do not believe any given truth about the world because of its own self-evident facticity; instead we believe certain assertions about the world with differing degrees of intensity based on how well they fit into the total network of other related ideas that we (and the communities in which we live) also hold to be true" (p. 56).

Although Murphy's epistemological views share some similarities to portions of the postmodern academy, the influence of her Anabaptist tradition leads her to diverge at important points. For instance, Murphy rejects Foucault's conclusion "that knowledge does not so much represent 'reality' as it does the interests of the social groups or individuals who have the power to impose their will on others" (Murphy and Ellis, 1996, p. 139). Instead she argues that these realities should lead us to the realization that "self-renunciation is not only the key to ethics—to orthopraxis; it is also the key to knowledge—to orthodoxy. Renunciation of the will to power is a prerequisite for seeking the truth" (Murphy and Ellis, 1996, p. 139). Once again, in Nancy Murphy's work "Christian scholarship can never be reduced to 'the life of the mind' alone" (Jacobsen and Jacobsen, 2004, p. 59). For the Anabaptist scholar, "knowledge, faith, and morality mingle and cohere in the context of our entire lives as scholars" (Jacobsen and Jacobsen, 2004, p. 59). In light of these facts, the Jacobsens suggest that the best possible integration model may occur by "living the questions" of intelligent faith rather than by trying to provide neat and tidy answers to all the questions of life.

Traditions, Worldviews, Narratives, and Practices: How Faith Shapes Reason

Each of these three traditions (Reformed, Anabaptist, and Roman Catholic) nurtured distinct communities with a distinct story, language, and practices about how the relationship between religious faith and scholarship should be understood. Each tradition also nurtured thinkers who developed or drew on particular resources to challenge the modern epistemological dominance of a particular concept of reason in the academy. Similar to various postmodern scholars, these thinkers and traditions made room for what might be called faith-informed scholarship by demonstrating the ways that human reason is often influenced by what they would respectively label one's worldview (Reformed), one's community narrative (Anabaptist), or one's tradition (Catholic). All three of these perspectives arose in reaction to the idea that there exists a form of reason that humans could achieve and employ that is ahistorical, universal, and unconditioned by the particularities of culture, religion, community, or human presuppositions.

Scholars from these religious traditions have also used these concepts, combined with an acceptance of pluralism, to challenge the academy to rethink its approach to religion and scholarship. As Marsden notes, historical scholars may agree over the details of the Battle of Little Bighorn, but they may disagree about whether it was "Custer's heroic last stand in a fight to bring peace to the American West" or "a triumph in the Native American fight to resist barbaric invaders." The differences involve "large-scale beliefs about what the world is, or should be, like" (1997, p. 62). In fact, Marsden's reply to the opening quote by Kuklick not surprisingly cites these three traditions as setting forth the claim that the distinctive religious tradition of universities and scholars has and does make a difference for scholarship. "It is easy to see how there might be (in fact there is) a Mennonite [or Anabaptist] view of political science or a Roman Catholic view of nuclear war, labor and capital or medical ethics. . . . In fact, conservative Presbyterians and other Reformed Christians, such as those at Calvin College, do have a view of human nature (and hence of anthropology in both its classic and modern senses) that distinguishes their outlook from the more optimistic views of many other Christians and secularists" (Marsden, 1997, p. 60). Others scholars making similar arguments also come from these traditions. The Jacobsens (2004) contend that realities such as "tradition-shaped thinking" should actually be considered "scholarly assets that allow us to discover or create things that others simply cannot see or do because their traditions are less attuned to these areas" (p. 78). Instead of relying on ideological blinders that undermine objective scholarship, they actually provide resources for scholarship that the scholar outside the tradition may not possess.

Likewise the Catholic historian James Turner (2002) in an essay entitled "Does Religion Have Anything Worth Saying to Scholars?" claims that the products of tradition-informed scholarship will not only help scholars immersed in a religious tradition but can also aid scholars outside religious traditions. In truth, "research in the humanities and social sciences will benefit if scholars today pay renewed attention to deploying within their different disciplines the *intellectual* tradition associated with Judaism, Christianity and Islam" (p. 16). In other words, by drawing on these intellectual resources "researchers in the various academic disciplines might actually discover, or rediscover, intellectual resources that enable them to work out new lines of thinking [and] develop approaches to problems that could not evolve from standard sources in their fields" (p. 18). The next two chapters provide examples of how individual scholars, networks, and institutions are attempting to demonstrate just these points. Although the individuals highlighted in this chapter demonstrate the importance of a particular religious tradition, the next chapter discusses what attention to the Christian tradition, broadly understood, has entailed for their scholarship.

Faith-Informed Scholarship Across the Disciplines

IF PRACTICAL RATIONALITY AND ACADEMIC THEORIZING are necessarily shaped by our identities and their associated intellectual traditions, what might be the practical implications for faith-informed scholarship? This chapter outlines what we regard as some consensus views from scholars answering this question. In addition, we offer some examples from those scholars who we believe demonstrate an effort to apply faith-informed approaches in the sciences, the social sciences, and the humanities.

The general case for faith-informed scholarship or opening "up space for a circumspect readmission of religious discourse into scholarship" generally involves two parts (Edwards, 2006, p. vii). First, as already discussed in the previous chapter, proponents argue that we must acknowledge that a person's worldview, communal identity narratives, or identified intellectual tradition will influence his or her scholarship in a variety of ways (Edwards, 2006; Clouser, 2005; Jacobsen and Jacobsen, 2004; Myers and Jeeves, 2003; Dovre, 2002; Sterk, 2002; Marsden, 1997; Sloan, 1994). For instance, Mark Edwards (2006) argues that we must recognize that disciplinary formation in the academy shapes who we are and how we look at the world. In the course of scholarly training, one acquires not only skills or practices but also a particular identity and an emotional attachment to that identity. Consequently, Edwards observes, "We find the orientation that a practice instills difficult to question and are apt to take it as self-evident. This orientation may also entail background or control beliefs that influence what we see, believe, and accept within our disciplinary work and beyond" (p. 60). Professional scholars in various disciplines come to see, understand, and experience the world in a certain way.

Even in the supposedly objective field of science, Thomas Kuhn (1970) and Michael Polanyi (2003) remind us of the various ways that a person's social, cultural, and ideological perspective influences one's research. In other words, everyone participates in worldview, narrative, or tradition-informed scholarship because all of us bring to scholarship a whole variety of identities and associated narratives and worldviews that influence the scholarly task.

Second, we cannot merely ignore or downplay those influences to make our scholarship more objective or neutral. Certainly if one discovers that ethnicity, race, or gender has influenced one's interpretation of a historical event (for example, European and not Native Americans are the ones who claim Columbus "discovered" America) when describing the event, the solution to such identity influence is often to find a commonly agreed-upon description that could be affirmed universally by all people (for example, Columbus sailed to America). Nonetheless, whereas modern scholars largely understood one's religious identity and beliefs (or other personal identities and beliefs) as negative factors that would alter objective research, faith-informed scholars recognize that the influence of one's identity and its associated narratives or traditions on one's way of understanding the world can be positive and not merely negative. Therefore, scholars argue that we should deepen our understanding of those influences. Those who engage in "faith-informed scholarship" are somewhat similar to feminists, Marxists, deconstructionists, pragmatists, and others who openly and honestly undertake scholarship with the recognition that the participant's identity influences and is influenced by the phenomena being studied. This recognition of participant-influenced scholarship offers a critical way, or perhaps even one of the best ways, to understand reality. The key difference is that religious scholars are working from a particular faith tradition that may inform and shape scholarship in a variety of distinct ways.

The Influence of Background Beliefs on Scholarship

Although scholars addressing the influence of a person's identity and its associated worldviews, narratives, and traditions on scholarship have identified numerous areas of influence, we will focus on six areas in particular that receive substantial attention: (1) scholarly agendas and motivations; (2) the choice of method; (3) the choice of data or phenomena to study; (4) the interpretive task; (5) the moral evaluation of the results; and (6) the overall influence of a faith tradition on a profession or tradition of inquiry.

Scholarly Agendas and Motivations

A person's identities and commitments, whether religious, nonreligious, or antireligious, often play an important role in that person's motivation for scholarly work, the applications perceived for the work, and a future scholar's attraction to a specific discipline or to a specific subject area in a discipline. George Marsden observes, "Christian motives often determine what fields people go into, what topics they study in those fields, and what questions they ask about those topics (1997, p. 64). Of course, nonreligious motives may also guide a person's choice of field. For example, David Myers and Malcolm Jeeves in *Psychology: Through the Eyes of Faith* (2003) note that ten times more psychologists than the average American deny the existence of God and wonder, "Do psychologists, like so many laypeople, tend to see the psychological account of human nature as competing with and elbowing out the religious account?" (2003, p. 13). Scholars also have views about what they think should be the best motives for entering a particular discipline or field, and religious convictions often play a role in forming those views. For example, the Jacobsens note that Christian academics not only should seek truth but also "seek truth in order to more intelligently love the world and every person in it" (2004, p. 159).

One's interest in specific issues in a discipline may also be guided by one's worldview (Jacobsen and Jacobsen, 2004; Myers and Jeeves, 2003; Marsden, 1997). Whether one picks a topic such as voting habits, smoking cessation, or moral education may be guided by religious convictions. In fact, one of the contributions of faith-informed scholarship, some argue, is that religious faith may also lead one to study subject areas that may be considered unimportant and thus neglected by others. For example, those undertaking faith-informed scholarship are those more likely to study the role that particular religious practices or beliefs may have on certain phenomena such as health or political decisions. Historian George Marsden's own study of religion in higher education is one clear example, and he himself points to others such as Princeton sociologist Robert Wuthnow, who has written *America and the Challenges of Religious Diversity* (2005), *All in Sync: How Music and Art Are Revitalizing American Religion* (2003), *Creative Spirituality: The Way of the Artist* (2001), *Growing Up Religious: Christians and Jews and Their Journeys of Faith* (1999), *After Heaven: Spirituality in America Since the 1950s* (1998), *Christianity and Civil Society: The Contemporary Debate* (1996a), and *Poor Richard's Principle: Recovering the American Dream Through the Moral Dimension of Work, Business, and Money* (1996b). Those most critical of faith-informed scholarship concede Marsden's point. For example, David Hollinger (2006, 2002) acknowledges that in the past the academy tended to dismiss or downplay the personal identity and circumstances of the individual inquirer. Today, he agrees, we should acknowledge the influence of a person's worldview on scholarly agendas and even recognize that such tradition-formed thinking may provide some distinctive intellectual resources for the university. Overall, it is recognized increasingly that both one's actual motives and one's understanding of what a scholar's ideal motives should be may have intellectual implications on one's scholarly work.

Method

Those who believe we should pay attention to the importance of faith-informed scholarship also point out that one's choice of method to obtain knowledge and the implementation of it can involve religious or antireligious considerations (Clouser, 2005; Jacobsen and Jacobsen, 2004; Myers and Jeeves, 2003; Marsden, 1997; Kuklick and Hart, 1997). Many criticisms religious scholars make of modern, objectivist methods of knowing echo the critiques of philosophers of science, feminists, and those in hermeneutics who argue that we must discard the old positivist model in which a detached observer can interpret mind-independent objects and acknowledge the participatory nature of knowing. They also make an important point about the significance of a person's religious worldview, however. George Marsden (1997) argues that scholars are often expected to adopt what Peter Berger has called "methodological atheism" when they approach a subject. When applied to the social sciences and humanities, however, it means "that humans and their cultures have to be regarded as nothing more than the products of natural processes" (p. 84). This conclusion rules out certain religious views a priori and ends up having important implications for our understanding of ethics and ethical knowledge. It becomes easier to assume or conclude ethical beliefs are nothing more than "the products of natural processes" (for a good example see Marc Hauser's *Moral Minds: How Nature Designed Our Universal Sense of Right and Wrong*, 2006). A method that is open to theism would radically change the possibilities.

Moreover, some scholars contend that certain kinds of virtues nurtured, not exclusively but often, in religious contexts (such as reverence, humility, and charity) can prove vital to both old and new methods of discovering knowledge (Jacobsen and Jacobsen, 2004; Schwehn, 2002a, 2002b, 1993; Sloan, 1994, 2002). For example, Sloan (1994) argues that if knowledge is participatory, the quality of knowledge we acquire about the world will depend on "the quality of the participants and the quality of their participation" (p. 236). In other words, "The possibility of a deepening of knowledge, thus, pre-supposes a constant working on oneself, on the full development of thinking, feeling, willing and character as essential to the fullness of cognition. The basic religious attitudes, for example, of wonder and reverence as readiness for what the other has to reveal, can, thereby, become more than mere inner feeling states. They can become primary cognitive organs without which nothing of genuine newness can be known" (p. 236). If Sloan is correct, the particular virtues or character qualities that religion helps produce in people may actually shape distinct tools for knowing. Similarly, scholars also maintain that one's worldview may also shape and inform the ethical standards that guide one's methods or the causes in which the methods are used even beyond the policies of an institutional review board (Jacobsen and Jacobsen, 2004; Myers and Jeeves, 2003; Marsden, 1997).

What Data or Phenomena Are Important?

One's identification of important phenomena or data to study when using a particular method is also an important matter influenced by one's worldview, narrative, or tradition of rationality. For example, will we study whether religion, a person's denominational affiliation, or particular metaphysical beliefs are important factors to consider when examining particular social phenomena? The answer to this question may depend on what Mark Edwards (2006) labels our "background beliefs" (p. 92). Marsden provides an example by referring to the story of Yale historian Harry Stout. Stout not only chose to study a religious subject (Puritanism), but his worldview also led him to see importance in different data that past secular historians such as Perry Miller and Edmund Morgan had left unexplored, that is, the Puritan sermon (p. 71). Similarly, the Jacobsens (2004) note that scholars who imbibed the theory of secularization "assumed human consciousness was inevitably moving away from religious ways of thought toward scientific ways of thought . . ." (p. 159). Consequently, religious ways of perceiving and understanding phenomena were a priori considered unimportant. Nancy Ammerman (2002) makes a related point with regard to sociology, noting that the earlier dominance of the secularization narrative in the field of sociology resulted in two problematic assumptions. The first assumption was that "education itself is a secular enterprise, and attention to the study of religion is attention misplaced" (p. 79). The second result was that "because many sociologists assumed that society was (or would soon become) secularized, attention has simply gone into other pursuits" (p. 79). Because, as we outlined in the first chapter, the secularization theory as traditionally espoused has been argued as problematic, social theorists ended up neglecting a field of study or falsely interpreting and presenting their own realm of knowledge based on faulty theorizing.

The Interpretive Task

Perhaps most important, scholars who recognize and support faith-informed scholarship contend that one's interpretations of phenomena or data will be influenced by one's worldview (Edwards, 2006; Clouser, 2005; Myers and Jeeves, 2003; Wright, 2003; Wolterstorff, 1999; Marsden, 1997; Gallagher and Lundin, 1989; Wells, 1989). Critics such as Hollinger also recognize that the interpretive task as well as the receptivity to particular interpretations of data involve beliefs about what should be considered legitimate knowledge. In other words, Hollinger sees that many engaged in faith-informed scholarship hope to change "the structure of plausibility taken for granted by the prevailing epistemic communities" (2002, p. 41).

This influence will occur at a variety of levels. At the most basic level, the conceptualization of important terms in one's interpretation will be influenced (Clouser, 2005). For example, Myers and Jeeves note that terms such as *mental and sexual health* or *self-actualization and fulfillment* cannot be interpreted without implicit assumptions about human well-being that are usually informed by one's worldview (2003, p. 13). Likewise, Marsden notes how the term *public good* often carries a host of worldview assumptions (1996, pp. 73–74). Second, the language of interpretation will carry ideological weight. As Myers and Jeeves (2003) point out, "whether we describe those who favor their own racial and national groups as 'ethnocentric' or as exhibiting strong 'group pride'; whether we view a persuasive message as 'propaganda' or 'education'" (p. 14) will depend on one's worldview. Third, the presuppositions guiding one's interpretation will be influenced by one's worldview. "Is it better to express and act on one's feelings, or to exhibit self-control?" (Myers and Jeeves, 2003, p. 13). The answer will likely depend on one's worldview.

Not surprisingly, it is in this area where most scholars suggest that religious faith can aid a person's scholarship. Faith-informed scholarship can help challenge taken-for-granted interpretations. In particular, Clouser (2005) and the Jacobsens point to how faith challenges various forms of reductionism—what the Jacobsens call "the attempt to explain—and, indeed sometimes to explain away—the complexity of the world by claiming that everything can ultimately be reduced to only one or a very few underlying mechanisms of cause and effect" (2004, p. 157). Although Marxists may sometimes reduce issues to economic struggle and biologists to the competition of selfish genes, people of faith, they contend, have important reasons for seeing the world as a unified whole. The result of this belief is the recognition that religiously derived or religiously based ideas may play as important a role in history and life as material factors.

Marsden and the Jacobsens also claim that religious faith can productively inform the metaphysical basis of one's interpretive framework, although they make this argument in different ways. The Jacobsens, similar to what we offered in the previous chapter, outline the contributions different traditions can and do make in interpretive scholarship. In contrast, Marsden discusses more general theological contributions that Christian scholars add that are rooted in doctrinal beliefs about creation, human anthropology, Jesus Christ's incarnation, and the Holy Spirit (or the dimension of spiritual reality). For instance, Marsden points out how the belief that we are creatures made in the image of a loving God provides an important foundation for human rights and moral principles. Mark Noll (2002) provides another concrete example in his essay "Teaching History as a Christian." He describes how his Christianity gives him what he calls "modest epistemological confidence" (p. 163). On one hand, Noll notes that his "increased confidence in the truthfulness of historic Christianity . . . has almost completely freed my mind from skepticism about the human ability to understand something about the past" (p. 163). On the other hand, it also serves as "a powerful check to blithe overconfidence in the capacities of historical knowledge" (p. 163). Christian doctrine helps him make sense of this important balance between two sides, "for if the heart of Christianity is the incarnation of God the Son, so the heart of historical knowledge is its duality between universal certainties and culturally specific particularities" (p. 164). What is noteworthy is how Noll views his Christian faith as providing a bridge between two disparate academic movements and schools of thought as they relate to his discipline.

Moral Evaluation of the Results

Advocates of paying attention to "faith-informed" scholarship also point to how the significance one attaches to scholarly findings and the moral framework one uses to evaluate them will always be guided by one's worldview or intellectual tradition (Alford, 2006; Alford and Naughton, 2001). If studies find Americans have fewer friends, then is it a social crisis or merely an interesting change that should not be evaluated as a negative phenomenon? The moral basis for an answer to such a question depends, at least partly, on one's prior moral views that are rooted in one's worldview. Similarly, C. John Sommerville (2006) describes how most university work must function with some ideal about what it means to be fully human. But how we come to an understanding of the moral ideals of a good human usually rests on or involves metaphysical ideas rooted in one's worldview. The role of worldviews in influencing moral ideals can also be cited in secular research. Myers and Jeeves (2003) observe how Kohlberg's theory of moral development has been criticized for merely being the moral ideal of "an articulate liberal secular humanist" or a "typical Western male" (p. 14).

The Historical Influence of Faith-Informed or Atheist-Informed Scholarship

Finally, when it comes to the academy, a discipline, or a particular subject, scholars who defend some form of faith-informed scholarship claim that such scholarship may have helped shape the practices and intellectual assumptions in the university, particular disciplines, or particular subjects (Turner, 2002). In fact, the academy would benefit by looking at how faith-informed scholarship helped form certain Western phenomena. For instance, James Turner argues that by drawing on these intellectual resources, "Researchers in the various academic disciplines might actually discover, or rediscover, intellectual resources that enable them to work out new lines of thinking [and] develop approaches to problems that could not evolve from standard sources in their fields" (p. 18).

An example of someone who makes such an argument for the academy as a whole is Mark Schwehn in *Exiles from Eden: Religion and the Academic Vocation in America* (1993). Although Schwehn's argument will be treated at length later, we merely wish to note how he undertakes what Turner suggests. Schwehn argues that the ethos of the modern university has in many ways been corrupted by modern approaches to the academic vocation that separate intellectual and moral virtue from academic practices. In contrast, he argues that we can learn from the faith-informed scholarly practices of early religious universities that understood spiritual virtues such as humility, faith, self-sacrifice, and charity as essential to the practices of the academy and the academic vocation (for a helpful outline of this early ethic, see Rüegg, 1992, pp. 32–34).

Another example of someone's demonstrating Turner's argument to the academy is historian C. John Sommerville's claim that "the basic assumptions of academic history come from Jewish and Christian sources" (2006, p. 129). In particular, he lists six of these assumptions:

> *(1) Modern historians always look for the most discreditable motive possible. They are not satisfied until they can find a selfish motive*

(the technical meaning of "depravity"). Roman historians would have preferred discovering human nobility, without seeing it as a mark of special grace. (2) We view history as linear, not as cyclical or chaotic or repetitive. When we speak of development (as we constantly do), we are in what is called the Deuteronomic tradition, an Old Testament theme. (3) We are interested in the judgment of history within our narratives. We would lose all interest in history, as would our students, if we could not take sides. (4) On the other hand, we are skeptical of the idea of progress, of some positive evolutionary principle built into history. We understand that all those "developments" cost something and may even bankrupt us. And that all history is equidistant from eternity. (5) We believe humans are free beings, moral agents. As we have said, there was once talk of making history a social science, resting on determinist assumptions. That has been given up, as impossible and uninteresting. (6) And we are great ironists. Irony, the amusement at seeing humans fail at being Godlike, is a very Christian perspective [p. 129].

Whether one judges the influence as positive or negative depends on one's worldview or intellectual tradition. Nonetheless, Sommerville suggests that we must recognize how Judaism and Christianity became embedded in the academy in this and other ways. Moreover, "consciousness raising" about the ways that these Jewish and Christian assumptions are instilled in the academy could help open up a discipline to ultimate questions, even if the answers to these questions often involve religious concepts.

Finally, scholars point to the importance of religious worldviews in the origins and shaping of ways of thinking about particular subjects or phenomena. Turner uses Charles Taylor's argument in *Sources of the Self* to demonstrate his point. Taylor (1989) argues that "it was Augustine who introduced the inwardness of radical reflexivity and bequeathed it to the Western tradition of thought. The step was a fateful one, because we have certainly made a big thing of the first-person standpoint . . ." (p. 131). Turner claims that if we take a participatory understanding of knowledge formation seriously, the Christian origins of a particular development should be interesting for more than just historians. The reason, he argues, is that because Augustine developed his standpoint as "a step on our road back to God," it is likely that this *telos* left some imprint on Western subjectivity. Turner concludes, "Were scholars to excavate and explore the specifically religious lineaments of subjectivity, they might help us better to understand prevailing notions of self-consciousness and inner life, whether in psychology, philosophy or other disciplines" (2002, p. 18). More recently, he cites how just war theory has provided a moral framework for thinking about war, the way that the concept of subsidiarity contributed to the constitutional arrangements of the European Union and the suggestion by Kathryn Tanner that Christian traditions could help provide alternative and more complex ways of defining property.

Specific Examples

To better understand some of the points listed above, it is helpful to consider some specific examples that highlight the work of prominent scholars from three representative areas of the academy—the sciences, the social sciences, and the humanities.

Science: John Polkinghorne

One of the most influential voices in the dialogue between science and religion remains John Polkinghorne, a physicist and Anglican priest. The titles of his recent works published by Yale University Press give some idea of the variety of topics he addresses: *Exploring Reality: The Intertwining of Science and Religion* (2005); *Science and the Trinity: The Christian Encounter with Reality* (2004); *The God of Hope and the End of the World* (2002); *Faith, Science and Under-standing* (2000); and *Belief in God in an Age of Science* (1998). As a survey of the entirety of his work is not possible, we will merely use his most recent book, *Exploring Reality,* to point out the ways that Polkinghorne undertakes a number of the activities that scholars have identified as being characteristic of "faith-informed scholarship."

First and foremost, Polkinghorne engages in a broad challenge to naturalistic reductionism by continually reminding readers of the limits of science. Part of the recognition, Polkinghorne relates in his introduction to *Exploring Reality,* actually involved his own career decisions. After twenty-five years as a physicist, Polkinghorne became a priest. He made the change not out of disillusionment with the field of physics but with the recognition that "science describes only one dimension of the many-layered reality within which we live, restricting itself to the impersonal and general, and bracketing out the personal and unique" (2005, p. ix). Because he shares a Catholic concern with the unity of knowledge and truth and notes that "even within its own domain science cannot yet tell a fully integrated story," he believes other disciplines and other approaches to reality are needed to gain a larger picture of reality (p. x).

Throughout the book he notes other limits of scientific theory and the need to turn to issues of metaphysics for explanatory answers. For example, when discussing how physicists decide between two different views of quantum probability suggested by Niels Bohr and David Bohm, Polkinghorne observes that the choice cannot be made on empirical grounds but must rest on "considerations such as economy, elegance and lack of contrivance" (2005, p. 14). His point is that "questions related to causality cannot be settled on strictly scientific grounds alone, but they call for acts of metaphysical assessment" (p. 14).

As a consequence of his recognition of the limits of empirical science and the need to make judgments based on metaphysical factors, he takes aim at naturalistic reductionists who find in their field an explanation for everything. In one chapter he reviews the uniqueness of humanity compared with animals and comments, "The fact that we share 98.4 percent of our DNA with chimpanzees shows the fallacy of genetic reductionism, rather than proving that we are only apes who are slightly different. After all, I share 99.9 percent of my DNA with Johann Sebastian Bach, but that fact carries no implication of a close correspondence between our musical abilities" (2005, p. 45). Likewise, when discussing the limits of overly materialistic accounts of evolutionary theory he writes, "Noetic dimensions of reality, such as those of the mathematical and the moral, are as significant to the human story as are the dimensions of materiality" (p. xiii). The source of these dimensions, Polkinghorne goes on to argue, "lies in the unifying will of the Creator, a fundamental insight that makes it intelligible not only that the universe is transparent to our scientific enquiry, but also that it is the arena of moral decision and the carrier of beauty. Those dimensions of reality, the understanding of whose character lies beyond the narrow explanatory horizon of natural science, are not epiphenomenal froth on the surface of a fundamentally material world, but they are gifts expressive of the nature of this world's Creator" (p. 58). Polkinghorne's use of theological doctrines such as creation also illustrates the way he believes that theological truths can contribute to scholarly understanding. His book *Science and the Trinity: The Christian Encounter with Reality* uses theological concerns and concepts such as the Trinity to frame and understand scientific discoveries.

Polkinghorne also believes religious knowledge can contribute to our knowledge in ethics, an area where the insights of science remain limited. Although science provides the knowledge to produce technology that then gives us new power, it proves unhelpful when it comes to the ethical application of this new power. Thus, in areas such as human cloning we must begin to turn to deeper metaphysical questions such as What is human nature? What is the soul? With regard to these questions, religious traditions do provide answers, although Polkinghorne points out that they do not always agree. For instance, although the official position of the Catholic Church appears to claim that the soul enters a person at conception, Polkinghorne takes what he terms a developmental view of the soul as something that forms and grows. "On this view, the moral status of the embryo is something that enhances as the fetus develops" (2005, p. 156). As can be seen from this short and inadequate overview, even a few samples of Polkinghorne's recent works provide evidence of the range of ways "faith-informed" scholarship can take place at a highly sophisticated level in the sciences.

Social Science: Rodney Stark and John Milbank

In *Sociology Through the Eyes of Faith*, David Fraser and Tony Campolo (1992) observe ironically that "sociologists should understand how their very opinions about society (and Christians) are socially influenced. Often this is not the case" (p. 13). Nancy Ammerman makes a similar point with regard to the whole theory of secularization. "Perhaps no single field has so clearly articulated and embodied the secularization of the academy as sociology" (2002, p. 76). Two well-known scholars, John Milbank and Rodney Stark, have undertaken efforts to help inform the discipline of sociology about its problematic story and the ways that naturalistic reductionism and faulty theorizing have corrupted its understanding of history and reality. The two scholars, however, undertake this deconstruction using different approaches.

John Milbank's well-known work, *Theology and Social Theory: Beyond Secular Reason,* starts with the very premises of sociology. In this work Milbank seeks to turn the tables on the past relationship between theology and social theory. Instead of allowing social theory to set the terms of the academic debate, Milbank seeks to overcome the accommodating "pathos of modern theology, and to restore in postmodern terms, the possibility of theology as a metadiscourse"—particularly in relation to social theory (1990, p. 1).

Milbank rejects the dominant empirical approach in sociology that claims that the purpose of sociology is merely to describe human relationships in society. Milbank, like the authors mentioned earlier, argues that every type of language, terminology, and method in sociology makes normative assumptions about human nature and the nature of human relationships. Every sociology therefore is rooted in theological or philosophical commitments and presuppositions. Christians moreover should be the first to realize that there is no social theory apart from the church. The church is a social theory. In other words, Christian social theory "is first and foremost an *ecclesiology,* and only an account of other human societies to the extent that the Church defines itself, in its practice, as in continuity and discontinuity with these societies" (1990, p. 380).

Only by acknowledging one's normative ideals about society can any sociology proceed. "Talk of 'a Christian sociology' or of 'theology as a social science' is not therefore, as silly as talk of 'Christian mathematic' (I suspend judgment here) precisely because there can be no sociology in the sense of a universal 'rational' account of the 'social' character of all societies, and Christian sociology is distinctive simply because it explicates, and adopts the vantage point of, a distinct society, the Church" (1990, pp. 380–381). The result, Milbank believes, will be that unlike traditional sociology, Christian sociology "refuses to treat reason and morality as ahistorical universals, but instead asks . . . how has Christianity affected human reason and human practice?" (1990, p. 381).

It is just such a question that has guided the work of the prominent sociologist Rodney Stark. Stark's pursuit of the question has been inspired not only by what he considers the faulty secularization thesis (1999) but also the materialistic view of history exemplified by Jared Diamond (1999) in his book *Guns, Germs and Steel*. Much like Max Weber, Stark has sought to challenge reductionistic historical and sociological interpretation by combining both historical and sociological methods to understand the importance of particular theological beliefs as a causal factor in history. In his opening work for this series, *One True God: The Historical Consequences of Monotheism* (2001), Stark sets forth the basic idea behind his agenda:

> . . . *[Although] many wonderful books have made the last decade an exciting time for anyone interested in broad assessments of the past, I was prompted by their example to write a reminder that history is not shaped by "material" factors alone. Granted, germs, geography, printing, sailing ships, steel, and climate have mattered, but probably none of them so much as human ideas about the gods. All of the great monotheisms propose that their God works through history, and I plan to show that, at least sociologically, they are quite right: that a great deal of history—triumphs as well as disasters— has been made on behalf of One True God. What could be more obvious? Well, one thing more obvious is that writing about the social effects of Gods just isn't done these days. It is widely assumed in scholarly circles that historical inquiries into such matters as the social consequences of monotheism are long outmoded and quite unsuitable [p. 1].*

In his next two books, *For the Glory of God: How Monotheism Led to Reformations, Science, Witch-Hunts, and the End of Slavery* (2003); and *The Victory of Reason: How Christianity Led to Freedom, Capitalism, and Western Success* (2005), Stark continued this agenda by arguing extensively for why beliefs about God played a unique causal and social role in the development of various social phenomena.

Humanities and Literature: Robert Lundin

Roger Lundin's works provide another example of a scholarly agenda guided and informed by a religious faith. His major works include *From Nature to*

Experience: The American Search for Cultural Authority (2005), *The Promise of Hermeneutics* (coauthored with Clarence Walhout and Anthony C. Thiselton, 1999), *Emily Dickinson and the Art of Belief* (1998), *The Culture of Interpretation: Christian Faith and the Postmodern World* (1993), *Literature Through the Eyes of Faith* (coauthored with Susan Gallagher, 1989), and *The Responsibility of Hermeneutics* (coauthored with Anthony C. Thiselton and Clarence Walhout, 1985).

It should be no surprise that as a professor of literature, of all the qualities mentioned above, his greatest attention is given to the importance of faith for interpretation of life and literature. In fact, Marsden uses Lundin's work *The Culture of Interpretation* to illustrate how Christian theological views about creation can challenge the transcendent self and alter perceptions of contemporary literary debates. Lundin describes how in these literary debates the human creator has risen to an exalted status by discarding God as both creator and authority. In the end, such a move leaves humans destructively making either their mind or body a god.

The distinctive influence of Lundin's faith perspective can also be found clearly in his most recent work, *From Nature to Experience.* Lundin describes the way that experience rather than nature has come to be prized as a source of authority in America. He notes how the title and content of Ralph Waldo Emerson's two works, *Nature* (1836) and "Experience" (1844), provide a helpful example of this shift. Similar to Stark, he contrasts his approach to literary history against the materialistic view proclaimed by Diamond. Lundin admits his views are guided by a "conviction currently out of intellectual favor" (2005, p. 4) and one at sharp odds with Diamond's interpretive presupposition. The idea is that "ideas have considerable power within history and, to some extent, over its course" (2005, p. 4). He does not want to discount the role of guns, germs, and steel; he merely wants greater balance.

Lundin is also not content merely to chronicle the change in America's reliance in authority from nature to experience; he also wants to explore its consequences, particularly the dubious effort "to extract from experience the very standards by which that experience is then to be judged" (2005, p. 9). Thus, he explores the limits of experience as a source of moral authority, especially with regard to specific creative and cultural activities such as biography and Biblical hermeneutics. Lundin then takes the step of using the Christian tradition and a Christian theologian to illuminate and to provide an answer to the limits of experience and the pragmatic tradition it has fostered:

> *In the end, where the pragmatic tradition concludes that experience must generate the very light that will guide us out of its own darkness,* From Nature to Experience *turns to an older tradition for illumination. This tradition speaks of the Word that was with God before the beginning of all things yet willingly "became flesh and dwelt among us." This is a way beyond illusion, and here is the promise of deliverance from the dream: "In him was life, and the life was the light of men. The light shines in the darkness, and the darkness has not overcome it" [Lundin, 2005, p. 14].*

For Lundin, to judge human experience we must look to a religious tradition that can be both in but not of it.

Overall, brief summaries such as these from Polkinghorne, Milbank, Stark, and Lundin fail to do justice to the sophistication of their work. But they do make clear the major point made by the proponents of faith-informed scholarship. Just as Marc Hauser or Jared Diamond's naturalistic outlook that is rooted in a particular intellectual tradition or worldview shapes their scholarship, faith perspectives can have a significant impact on certain aspects of one's work; such faith-informed scholarship "has a viable and important role to play within a truly diverse academy" (Marsden, 2002, p. 42). The next chapter shows how religious colleges and universities are attempting to give more attention and support to this vision.

Faith-Informed Scholarship and the Practices of Networks and Institutions

ALTHOUGH RELIGIOUS TRADITIONS and individuals have nurtured general approaches to knowledge that have led to the contemporary resurgence and possibility of faith-informed scholarship, the question of how institutions of higher education seek to incorporate these intellectual developments also proves to be vitally important. As various scholars have noted, secularization became institutionalized in colleges and universities through a host of concrete institutional practices, not merely through intellectual means (Burtchaell, 1998; Marsden, 1994). College and university leaders renamed Bible or theology departments to religion or religious studies, and their courses were no longer required. They no longer required chapel—or disbanded it altogether. They abolished religious membership requirements for faculty and severed governance and financial support from sponsoring denominations or churches. Finally (and probably only in the end), they secularized the public rhetoric and official visions of their institutions. The manner in which church and parachurch organizations have come to ring the perimeters of so many college campuses eventually became symbolic of the life of the university as a whole and scholarship in particular.

As we discussed in the first chapter, near the turn of the twenty-first century, various scholars questioned the exclusion of religious faith from matters of scholarship. And as we noted in the next two chapters, religious traditions and scholars have nurtured coherent understandings of Christian identity, tradition, and reasoning that are beginning to bear increasing fruit and gain further attention. Scholars have contended, however, that if faith-informed scholarship is to be more than a vision produced by philosophers, historians, and theologians associated with certain religious traditions, the connection rekindled between religious faith and scholarship must also involve recovering old or creating new methods of institutionalizing this relationship (Jacobsen and Jacobsen, 2004; Benne, 2001; Marsden, 1997). This chapter will explore the organizational and institutional means religious schools and scholars have sought to nurture and sustain a vital relationship between religious faith and scholarship.

The first section offers an overview of contemporary networks of Christian colleges and universities that seek to provide their members with the resources they need to cultivate environments on their respective campuses where religious faith and scholarship can come into profitable relationships. The second section discusses particular institutional practices that religious schools have developed that also attempt to nurture faith-informed missions and scholarship. The third section briefly discusses the important scholarly organizations outside religious colleges and universities that provide a forum for addressing issues pertaining to faith and scholarship.

Old and New Networks of Religious Colleges and Universities

In the past, particular religious traditions established denominational networks for their own institutions. Perhaps the largest network of schools in a particular religious tradition is the Association of Catholic Colleges and Universities, with more than 220 member institutions. Founded in 1899, it seeks to "promote Catholic higher education by supporting the member institutions, especially with reference to their Catholic mission and character and to serve as The Voice of Catholic Higher Education in the United States" (http://www.accunet.org/). It accomplishes its mission by publishing its own journal, *Current Issues in Catholic Higher Education,* organizing various national meetings, and providing resources for scholarship pertaining to peace and justice as well as other matters related to Catholic social teaching. Colleges and universities related to a particular Catholic religious order have their own subnetworks. For example, the Association for Jesuit Colleges and Universities (AJCU) seeks to provide a host of information reflecting the needs of its twenty-eight member institutions (http://www.ajcu.net.edu). The AJCU Web site describes how the Jesuit heritage of these institutions is being fostered. For instance, Boston College currently has in place a vice president for mission and ministry who reports to the president, a Jesuit spiritual formation center, and a host of professional development initiatives for faculty members.

Similar networks of schools exist in mainline Protestant denominations such as the Lutheran (http://www.lutherancolleges.org/), Presbyterian (http://www.apcu.net/), United Methodist (http://www.gbhem.org/gbhem/colleges.html), and Baptist denominations (http://www.baptistschools.org/) to name but a few. Although many of these Protestant denominational networks provide resources to strengthen the institutions as a whole or the denominational identity in particular, consistent with the role of the mainline Protestant tradition in scholarship, few of them give direct attention to nurturing distinctly religious forms of scholarship or what we have called "faith-informed scholarship."

In contrast to these mainline Protestant denominational networks, one of the interesting recent developments is the establishment of networks of institutions that reach across denominational lines and focus more intensely on matters of faith and learning for students and faith-informed scholarship among faculty. These efforts reflect a trend identified by sociologists of religion some time ago who find new partnerships developing among religious groups that focus less on denominational distinctiveness and more on common Christian purposes and interests (Hunter, 1991; Wuthnow, 1989). Colleges and universities seeking to develop a core institutional identity reflective of an enduring connection between religious faith and scholarship have benefited greatly from these new sets of networks that transcend particular denominations or Christian traditions. Two networks are considerably noteworthy in this regard.

The Council for Christian Colleges and Universities
In 1971 a group of ten small Evangelical colleges joined together to form the Christian College Consortium. Its founding document noted that one of the stated purposes of the group was "to encourage and support scholarly

research among Christian scholars for the purpose of integrating faith and learning" (Patterson, 2001, p. 32). This consortium and its purpose would later play an important role in the founding and mission of the Council for Christian Colleges and Universities, which was originated in 1976 with thirty-eight member institutions. Today the Council includes 105 member institutions and seventy-one affiliate members. The two primary points of difference between the two groups are that member institutions need to "offer comprehensive undergraduate curricula rooted in the arts and sciences" and "hire as full-time faculty members and administrators only persons who profess faith in Jesus Christ" (http://www.cccu.org/about/about.asp?contentID=7). In contrast, affiliate members do not need to meet these two criteria but "seek to honor Jesus Christ in their academic missions" (http://www.cccu.org/about/affiliates.asp).

Despite their connections to particular Protestant denominations, the current list of 105 member institutions and most affiliate members reflects what one might describe as the evangelical segment of Protestantism. In fact, a statement of faith from the National Association of Evangelicals served as the statement of faith for member institutions of the Christian College Consortium (Patterson, 2001). In addition, similar to the Christian College Consortium's early mission statement, the mission of the CCCU is "to advance the cause of Christ-centered higher education and to help our institutions transform lives by faithfully relating scholarship and service to biblical truth" (http://www.cccu.org/about/about.asp).

The CCCU advances the scholarly aspect of its mission through a variety of means such as sponsoring conferences and book series related to the integration of faith and learning. As far back as 1973, the Lilly Endowment provided the consortium with external funding to support what became known as Faith/Learning/Living Seminars. These seminars "explored not only issues related to integration, but also the historical, educational, biblical, and philosophical foundations of the Christian liberal arts college" (Patterson, 2001, p. 34). Currently based in Washington, D.C., the CCCU's host of programs and publications also continue to support the Christian identity on the campuses of both its members and its affiliates. For example, recent conferences hosted by the CCCU include "Search for the Moral Hero: Explorations of

Social, Political and Ethical Justice in Cinema," "Christianity, Culture, and Diversity in America," and "Faith in Psychology and Counseling."

Since the 1980s, the CCCU has also worked to develop at least two different series of publications intended to be used by faculty members in college courses. All these books reflect serious attempts to produce faith-informed scholarship. In partnership with Harper San Francisco, "Through the Eyes of Faith" was the first series to be developed. It sought to address faith and learning in a variety of academic disciplines, including biology, business, history, literature, music, psychology, and sociology. For example, in *Music Through the Eyes of Faith,* Harold M. Best attempted "to celebrate the uniqueness of music making as part of the larger world of human creativity, and to hold that music making is subordinate to, and informed by, the larger doctrines of creation, worship, offering, faith, grace, stewardship, redemptive witness, excelling, and love" (1993, p, 7). In a more recent partnership with Baker Academic, the CCCU developed the "Renewed Minds" series, which offers guides to individuals seeking to think critically about matters involving faith and learning. Although more interdisciplinary in nature than the first series, books in the "Renewed Minds" series are also designed to be used as textbooks. Recent titles include William Ringenberg's *The Christian College: A History of Protestant Higher Education in America* (2006), Quentin J. Schultze's *Here I Am: Now What on Earth Should I Be Doing?* (2005), Harry Lee Poe's *Christianity in the Academy: Teaching at the Intersection of Faith and Learning* (2004), and Clifford Williams's *The Life of the Mind: A Christian Perspective* (2002).

Lilly Fellows Program in Humanities and the Arts

The Lilly Fellows Program in the Humanities and the Arts (LFP) was established during the 1990–91 academic year as a network seeking to develop forms of institutional identity that foster relationships between religious faith and scholarship. Based at Valparaiso University, the mission of the Lilly Fellows Program is to "renew and enhance the connections between Christianity and the academic vocation at church-related colleges and universities" (http://www.lillyfellows.org/about_lilly_fellows.htm). In essence, the LFP serves as a response to the wave of interest created in revitalizing the spiritual dimension of the academic vocation that resulted from the publication of

Mark R. Schwehn's *Exiles from Eden: Religion and the Academic Vocation in America* (1993), discussed elsewhere.

Whereas the majority of the CCCU's member institutions represent evangelical Protestantism, member institutions of the LFP are far more diverse. Their eighty-one member institutions include schools in the evangelical movement but also mainline Protestant and Catholic schools. In addition to greater religious diversity, the LFP member institutions also represent a greater range of institutional types. For example, research universities such as Baylor University, Boston College, and the University of Notre Dame and liberal arts colleges such as the College of the Holy Cross and Davidson College are all members of the LFP.

Beyond religious and organizational diversity, perhaps the biggest difference between the CCCU and the LFP is the LFP's vision for a network that can nurture integrated understandings of the academic vocation. This program has primarily sought to do so through two particular means. First, LFP offers a handful of scholars the opportunity to be part of a two-year postdoctoral teaching fellowship program. Scholars within two years of completing their respective terminal degree are eligible to apply. More important, "Fellows are selected from applicants who evince an interest in the relationship between Christianity and the academic vocation and are considering a career at church-related colleges or universities" (http://www.valpo.edu/lillyfellows/fellowship.html). Fellows are provided with an opportunity to teach courses at Valparaiso while also establishing a research agenda. Second, the LFP provides funding to member institutions to establish or strengthen faculty mentoring programs. According to the LFP, these mentoring programs seek to "encourage new faculty as well as veteran faculty to understand and share the ethos of the school, to grow to love the questions that the institution holds dear, and to consider the importance of fundamental matters concerning the relationship between higher learning and the Christian faith" (http://www.lillyfellows.org/index.htm). Institutions recently receiving awards include Concordia University (Nebraska), Eastern Mennonite University, Loyola Marymount University, and Presbyterian College.

Like the CCCU, the LFP also supports a number of conferences. The first type of conference hosted by the Lilly Fellows Network is its national conference.

It gathers official representatives of all the network colleges and universities "to consider a significant issue of faith and learning, exchange ideas and practices regarding their mission, and foster the whole range of Network programs and activities" (http://www.lillyfellows.org/lfp_national_conferences. htm). For example, the title of a recent national conference at Xavier University (Ohio) was "A Blessed Heritage: The Contributions of Church-Related Higher Education." The second type of conference the LFP supports is research conferences. Member institutions are offered the opportunity to apply to not only host the conference but also receive funding to support the conference. Although the conferences have historically proved to be topical and interdisciplinary in nature, their common purpose is to foster and promote "research that addresses issues of faith and learning, Christian practices of teaching, the relationship of religion and the academic disciplines, the relationship of the sacred and the secular, or other aspects of church-related higher education" (http://www.lillyfellows.org/research_conferences.htm).

These networks appear to be successful for at least two particular reasons. On one hand, they encourage their member institutions to take their institutional religious identities and histories seriously and in turn relate them to their aspirations for scholarship. For example, both group's efforts recognize that the Reformed theological tradition is inextricable from the scholarly aspirations of an institution such as Calvin College. On the other hand, these networks also encourage scholars to view their aspirations in the comparative light of other religious traditions. As a result, programs supported by the CCCU serve as a means of drawing together scholars from a Reformed institution such as Calvin College and a Wesleyan institution such as Seattle Pacific University. Likewise, programs supported by the LFP serve as a means of drawing together scholars from a Reformed institution such as Calvin College and a Catholic institution such as the University of Notre Dame. In the end institutional networks such as the CCCU and the LFP deepen a particular college or university's understanding of its own heritage while also helping it learn lessons from other traditions. As a result, this cross-fertilization has overall had a positive impact on the ability of colleges and universities to develop forms of institutional identity that foster relationships between religious faith and scholarship.

Religious Faith and Scholarship: Institutional Practices

Categories of religious traditions can tell us something about how a particular college or university fosters an environment in which religious faith and learning can enter constructive relationships with one another. Networks of institutions can provide particular colleges and universities with the resources they need to meet this challenge. But if one wants to know how such relationships are really developed, one must look at the practices in place at particular institutions. Although the relationship between religion and scholarship has seen increased attention in the academy as a whole, the majority of public and even private research universities have made no effort to date to institutionalize such efforts. A number of recent studies, however, have attempted to outline and examine the practices of specific colleges and universities from a variety of religious traditions that are attempting to keep the faith (see, for example, the discussion of specific institutions in Poe, 2004; Dovre, 2002; Benne, 2001; and Hughes and Adrian, 1997).

Robert Benne's typology (2001) provides probably the most helpful outline for understanding, categorizing, and analyzing the approaches of various schools regarding religion and the practices of an institution in general. Benne examines eight aspects of an institution's life: (1) public relevance of religious vision, (2) public rhetoric, (3) membership requirements, (4) religion/theology department and religion/theology required courses, (5) chapel, (6) ethos, (7) support by church, and (8) governance (p. 49). Although Benne's typology clearly includes some distinctly Protestant aspects, particularly its emphasis on chapel, his categories still prove helpful when studying the diverse ways Christian institutions attempt to keep faith with their tradition.

Benne uses his typology to place schools at various degrees of faithfulness to their tradition (orthodox, critical mass, intentionally pluralist, and accidentally pluralist). As the types move from orthodox to accidentally pluralist, they become more secular or permissive. For example, orthodox schools "want to assure that the Christian account of life and reality is publicly and comprehensively relevant to the life of the school by requiring that all adult members of the ongoing academic community subscribe to a statement of belief"

(2001, p. 50). Critical mass institutions, however, "do not insist that all members of the community be believers in their tradition or even believers in the Christian tradition [but instead] insist that a critical mass of adherents from their tradition inhabit all the constituencies of the educational enterprise—board, administration, faculty, and student body" (2001, p. 50). In the end he argues that some schools can and are resisting secularization.

Although Benne's typology offers an overview of an institution's practices regarding faith, his outline does not focus on the ways that an institution seeks to integrate religion and scholarship beyond certain curricular requirements for students or religious membership requirements for faculty. Our intention in this section is more focused. Though not exhaustive, we offer details concerning what some of the most common institutional practices are that attempt to nurture faith-informed scholarship. Some of these practices are unique to colleges and universities seeking to foster environments where religious faith and scholarship can come into constructive relationships with one another. And some of these practices, albeit slightly revised, are common to institutions that take seriously the manner in which they offer professional development opportunities to the members of their communities.

Hiring for Religious and Scholarly Mission

For many schools the challenge of institutionalizing a relationship between religious faith and scholarship begins with the hiring process. Candidates at most of the institutions that are members of the CCCU and the LFP seek to hire faculty members and administrators with an understanding of, or at least an openness to learning, how to draw connections between their faith and their scholarly efforts (Braskamp, Trautvetter, and Ward, 2006). Because the preponderance of candidates seeking appointments in colleges and universities that want to institutionalize the relationship between religious faith and learning earned terminal degrees from secular research universities, an openness to learn more about such efforts has become the key in hiring for mission. Although searches for positions usually begin with the department, many of the colleges Benne mentions as having "quality with soul" such as Baylor University, Calvin College, St. Olaf College, the University of Notre Dame, and Valparaiso University require new tenure-track faculty to interview with the president or chief academic officer (Benne, 2001; see also the schools described in Hughes and Adrian, 1997). Such officials are usually thought to have the institutional responsibility for determining whether a candidate is truly open to scholarship that takes into account the university's mission, not merely the interests of a particular academic department or field.

Some schools are also quite explicit about ways that ideal candidates can contribute to the university's mission. Some of the interests Mark Roche suggests for the ideal candidate at the University of Notre Dame include "the infusion of the liberal arts ideal with a spiritual dimension; the goal of educating the whole person; the development of interconnections among the disciplines; the interrelation of learning and morality and of reason and faith; and . . . the ideal of service to the world [as well as] . . . the dignity of the human person and a sacramental vision that finds divine presence in the world; the unity of knowledge and an openness to the mystery of transcendence; universal human rights and international social justice; and respect for intellectual community and for the wisdom of the ages" (M. Roche, quoted in Benne, 2001, p. 124).

As mentioned, a few colleges and universities have developed offices of institutional mission and identity to help with such efforts. Because these offices do more than simply seek to develop an institutional awareness of the development of relationships shared by religious faith and learning, they do provide resources to individuals on their campuses conducting searches. For example, the Office for Mission Effectiveness at Villanova University offers the members of its community a "Guide for Faculty Search Committees: Mission Centered Hiring." This document offers individuals leading search committees sample topics to be probed with individual candidates. Such topics include how a candidate resonates with the mission of the university as well as how his or her "work fits[s] in with the academic mission of Villanova University" (http://www3.villanova.edu/mission/). As part of its role at Marquette University, the Office of Mission and Identity "offers individual and group opportunities for reflection and discussion on vocation and the integration of mission with daily work" (http://www.marquette.edu/umi/about/index.shtml). When it comes to hiring, search committees at Marquette are encouraged to ask questions such as "While teaching performance and qualifications are central to our educational mission, we are also part of a religious tradition here at Marquette. What are your thoughts about the relationship between faith and reason in the academic environment?" (http://www.marquette.edu/umi/mission/interview.shtml). Through such questions, communities such as Villanova and Marquette seek to include information about a candidate's perceptions concerning the relationship shared by religious faith and scholarship in the hiring process.

Other universities have offered financial incentives to departments to hire candidates who address issues of religion and scholarship or have created distinguished professor positions for faculty to address matters of faith and scholarship. For example, the provost and academic deans at the University of Notre Dame offered departments grants to identify and recruit Catholic scholars who seek to address matters of faith in their scholarship, and Baylor University established twenty new distinguished professor positions around the university that they then sought to fill largely with faculty who focus on the intersection between faith and learning (Benne, 2001; see also http://www.baylor.edu/provost/index.php?id=001134). Although hiring faculty with a particular religious identity or who must affirm a particular confessional statement is often criticized as being too rigid or narrow (Wolfe, 2000), maintaining the particular theological heritage and traditions of a religious college often starts with requiring a faculty member to affirm the particular mission and identity of the institution (Litfin, 2004).

Mentoring New Faculty Members and Administrators

The inclination to hire for mission is usually just the beginning of a professional development process for new faculty members. In *Mentoring for Mission: Nurturing New Faculty at Church-Related Colleges* (2003), Caroline J. Simon, Laura Bloxham, and Denise Doyle note that scholarship on church-related campuses should not only be of the highest scholarly order but also reflect the needs and interests of the church. In the end, the key to developing habits leading to such efforts is mentoring. "Well-designed mentoring programs lead to more confident junior faculty members who understand their home institutions and enthusiastically contribute to institutional mission" (p. 2). Similar convictions have led many schools to develop programs that seek to develop mentoring opportunities in a host of ways. One of the most critical is to work to identify an individual mentor for new faculty members and administrators. A person serving as a mentor is usually a senior colleague who understands the pressures placed on his or her new colleague. To facilitate open dialogue, the mentor often serves as a direct or even indirect supervisor for his or her new colleague.

Personal mentoring programs have become common in the academy. They certainly can have a positive impact on developing the scholarly habits of new colleagues. Colleges and universities seeking to institutionalize a relationship between religious faith and learning, however, realize that new colleagues also need a venue to interact with some of their most accomplished senior colleagues. Two particular practices are often used in pursuit of such an end. First, retreats are used as a means of providing a concentrated set of experiences for an institution's new colleagues. Faculty members and administrators are taken for a week or two at a time to a location beyond the campus to focus on developing the habits and practices necessary to develop the relationship shared by religious faith and learning. For example, Baylor University has offered new faculty members and faculty members in particular colleges the opportunity to attend a week-long retreat during the summer. During the retreat participants are asked to read and discuss the works of Christian scholars past and present on the topic of vocation. The retreat also provides participants with the opportunity to read and interact with scholars engaged in some form of faith-informed scholarship such as Mark Schwehn, Dorothy Bass, and C. Stephen Evans. Examples of similar collections of readings used at other institutions include John C. Haughey's *Revisiting the Idea of Vocation: Theological Explorations* (2004), William C. Placher's *Callings: Twenty Centuries of Christian Wisdom on Vocation* (2005), and Mark R. Schwehn and Dorothy C. Bass's *Leading Lives that Matter: What We Should Do and Who We Should Be* (2006).

Second, perhaps more popular than retreats for new faculty members and administrators are special classes or seminars. Administrators at Catholic schools cited this approach as one way they help scholars relate their work to the Catholic mission of the institution (Morey and Piderit, 2006). New colleagues are given release time to participate in an ongoing effort over the course of a semester to help them explore the relationship shared by religious faith and scholarship. Some campuses offer such courses during the academic year. For example, Azusa Pacific University offers a two-semester course sequence. The first course, Faith Integration and Curriculum Development, introduces colleagues to ways religious faith can be integrated in not only their teaching but also "formal research" (Hoff, 2004, p. 10). "For those who opt to continue [with the second course], Theological Research across the academic disciplines immerses them in rigorous scholarly theological research" (2004, p. 10). Some campuses offer courses during abbreviated terms in January or May. For instance, faculty members and administrators at Calvin College are given a chance to take such a course during the May term. The basis for one such course was a collection of readings by Nicholas Wolterstorff entitled *Keeping Faith: Talks for New Faculty at Calvin College,* which provides not only an overview of the histories of the Reformed tradition and Calvin College but also how those histories invite new colleagues into the understanding that "God at creation gave to humanity the mandate to develop the potentials of creation. The development of the academic disciplines is seen as helping to carry out that mandate" (1989, p. 53).

Promotion and Tenure

At colleges and universities that seek to offer faculty members and administrators ways to integrate faith and learning such as schools in the CCCU, accountability for such an understanding in a formal sense usually comes at some point. For administrators, questions often exist on annual evaluation forms concerning how religious faith is evident in the decisions they made and the curricular or cocurricular programs they developed. For faculty members, questions usually exist on teaching evaluation forms asking students and peer evaluators to assess the ability of a particular faculty member to demonstrate the relationship shared by religious faith and scholarship in a particular course.

With regard to the scholarship of discovery, several colleges and universities have found ways to incorporate the need for faculty members to demonstrate the relationship shared by religious faith and scholarship in the promotion and tenure process. For example, in its *Handbook for Teaching Faculty,* Calvin

College states that for faculty members "it is not sufficient, for example, simply to keep up with developments in one's field. It is also necessary to be attentive to changes in culture and society that impinge on one's scholarly field and to subject them to critical assessment in the light of Christian commitment" (http://www.calvin.edu/admin/provost/fac_hb/chap_3/3_6.htm). It should be noted that it also defers to the "department along with the Professional Status Committee to identify the kinds of publication or production that constitute an adequate program of scholarship for reappointment and tenure, and to specify the ways in which such scholarly work can be appropriately evaluated and documented" (http://www.calvin.edu/admin/provost/fac_hb/chap_3/3_6.htm). In a similar manner, Messiah College defers to its schools and academic departments to determine what defines scholarship, but it also requires all faculty members, as part of their application for promotion and tenure, to develop a paper of publishable quality that demonstrates their understanding of the relationship shared by religious faith and scholarship in their respective fields. At Wheaton College, "all Faculty are expected to complete a Faith and Learning Paper. The Completion of the Paper is necessary for promotion and essential for tenure consideration" (Wheaton College, 2006).

Other Support Structures

Some colleges and universities have set up more particular offices or institutes in the university to enhance and promote faith-based scholarship. Perhaps most common among Catholic schools are the offices of mission and identity that have emerged at universities such as Marquette and Villanova. Other universities have created particular institutes to address matters of faith and scholarship. For example, Baylor University established the Institute of Faith and Learning, which sponsors speakers, dialogue sessions, and academic conferences addressing matters of faith and learning (http://www3.baylor.edu/IFL/). Similar centers are found at other colleges noted for their work on religion and scholarship such as Calvin College, Gordon College, Pepperdine University, and Whitworth College. The University of Notre Dame boasts perhaps the most extensive group of centers and institutes that focus on matters related to faith and scholarship, including the Cushwa Center for the Study of American Catholicism, the Center for Social Concern, the Center for Ethics and

Religious Values in Business, the Erasmus Institute, the Jacques Maritain Center, and the Reilly Center for Science, Technology, and Values.

Religion and Scholarship: Networks of Scholars and Professional Associations

Outside the university, the reemergence of interest in religiously informed scholarship has been tremendously aided by the growth of various Christian scholarly associations (see, for example, Poe, 2004; Marsden, 1997; Noll, 1994). The Society of Christian Philosophers, created in 1978, is often cited as the most prominent example. Various associations have been created for literature (the Conference on Christianity and Literature), history (the Conference on Faith and History), and science (the American Scientific Affiliation). Exhibit 1 lists several of these organizations. Many of them have their own journals, Web sites, and scholarly conferences (for additional information about these organizations, see the appendix in Poe, 2004, pp. 185–192).

For instance, the Society of Christian Psychology recently held a conference, "Faith and Psychology in Counseling," whose stated purpose was to help scholars learn to overturn "the opposition of faith to many other aspects of human life: reason and knowing in general, empirical research, psychological theory, counseling, the mental health profession, and morality and good works" (http://www.cccu.org/conferences/eventID.400/conference_detail.asp).

The questioning of secularization and the revival of interest in religion and scholarship have resulted in a renewed effort among religious colleges and universities to find ways to strengthen their efforts to sustain faith-informed scholarship. Increasing attention to broad Christian networks, hiring and training faculty with an interest and specialization in faith-informed scholarship, and creating institutional structures that support various types of faith-informed scholarship have arisen at many religious colleges and universities. The efforts of individual scholars such as John Polkinghorne, Rodney Stark, John Milbank, and Robert Lundin are undoubtedly significant. But one can only assume that their efforts are in some way or another also the by-products of being part of institutions or networks that helped to shape not only the questions they asked but also the answers they offered. One cannot underestimate

EXHIBIT 1
Christian Professional Associations

Affiliation of Christian Biologists
Affiliation of Christian Geologists
American Scientific Affiliation
American Society of Church History
Association of Christian Collegiate Media
Association of Christian Economists
Association of Christian Engineers and Scientists
Association of Christian Librarians
Association of Christians in Mathematical Sciences
Association of Christians Teaching Sociology
Canadian Society of Christian Philosophers
Christian Association for Psychological Studies
Christian Business Faculty Association
Christian Educators Association, International
Christian Fellowship of Art Music Composers
Christian Foresters Fellowship
Christian Legal Society
Christian Medical and Dental Society
Christian Nuclear Fellowship (Nuclear Science and Technology)
Christian Performing Artists' Fellowship
Christian Pharmacists Fellowship International
Christian Sociological Society
Christian Theological Research Fellowship
Christian Veterinary Mission
Christians in the Arts Networking
Christians in Political Science
Christians in Theatre Arts
Christians in the Visual Arts
Conference on Christianity and Literature
Conference on Faith and History
Engineering Ministries International
Fellowship of Christian Librarians and Information Specialists
Health Physics Society Christian Fellowship
Network of Christian Anthropologists
Neuroscience Christian Fellowship

Exhibit 1 (*Continued*)

North American Association of Christians in Social Work
North American Christian Foreign Language Association
Nurses Christian Fellowship
Religious Communication Association
Society of Christian Philosophers
Society of Christian Psychology

how matters of socialization influence the worldviews of individual scholars and in turn the scholarship they produce. The question of what difference faith makes for scholarship in light of current conversations about academic freedom is the focus of the next chapter.

Faith-Informed Scholarship and the Practice of Academic Freedom

DISCUSSIONS ABOUT ACADEMIC FREEDOM and its relationship to faith-informed scholarship are often conducted in the narrative framework of liberal education. In this framework, the metaphysical (or ontological) beliefs affirmed by a university should not impinge on a scholar's research. Martha C. Nussbaum's *Cultivating Humanity: A Classical Defense of Reform in Liberal Education* (1997) illustrates such an understanding. Nussbaum develops a comparison between the practices of academic freedom exhibited at the University of Notre Dame and at Brigham Young University (BYU). Both institutions are the products of religious traditions—the Roman Catholic tradition as embodied by the Congregation of the Holy Cross and the Church of Jesus Christ of Latter Day Saints, respectively. Nussbaum contends, however, that Notre Dame and BYU "lie in many ways at opposite ends of a spectrum" when it comes to matters such as academic freedom (1997, p. 261). In Nussbaum's opinion, "Notre Dame has constructed a genuinely religious education within a first-rate research university with strong guarantees of academic freedom" (1997, p. 261). In contrast, BYU is "a university far more disposed to restrict scholarship and inquiry in the name of religious belief" (p. 262). Not surprisingly, Nussbaum's denigration of a university that takes metaphysical views seriously is consistent with her own metaphysical agnosticism. Although Nussbaum states, "I take my relation to Judaism very seriously, gave my daughter a religious education, and am a member of a synagogue," she also admits "I focus on religion's moral and social content and am uncertain about metaphysical belief" (p. 262).

More recently, religious scholars are noting that enforcing metaphysical agnosticism is hardly a neutral position (see, for example, Plantinga, 2000; Smith, 2004). This conclusion has led some religious scholars to set forth alternative approaches to academic freedom that are not tied so directly to metaphysical agnosticism. As we will demonstrate in this chapter, for these scholars understanding the relationship between metaphysics and academic freedom leads to an ability to understand the full nature of the relationship shared between faith-informed scholarship and academic freedom.

Defining Academic Freedom

Defining the specific nature of academic freedom has proved difficult. For example, in the introduction to his edited volume with Ellen Schrecker entitled *Regulating the Intellectuals: Perspectives on Academic Freedom in the 1980s,* Craig Kaplan says that among the contributors "there is little consensus regarding the meaning of academic freedom although there is agreement that it is something worth protecting" (1983, p. 6).

Perhaps the most comprehensive treatment of academic freedom from a faith-informed perspective is offered by Anthony J. Diekema in *Academic Freedom and Christian Scholarship* (2000). In this work, Diekema seeks to explain how metaphysics relates to academic freedom by distinguishing between personal or individual academic freedom and institutional or corporate academic freedom. Diekema realizes that academic freedom is not simply a moral practice exercised by an individual but also an institutional practice and that the two share an enduring connection. In relation to the personal or individual definition of academic freedom, Diekema contends that "academic freedom is a foundational principle granted only within the academy and designed to protect the professors—whose lives are dedicated to conserving and extending the realm of knowledge—from all of those forces, both internal and external [that] tend to prevent them from meeting all of the obligations of the professional office in the pursuit of truth" (2000, p. 85). Diekema's definition recognizes professors are the ones who have given their lives to the generation and dissemination of knowledge. To fulfill such a charge, they need to work in an environment that seeks to protect them from forces of a varied nature that may seek to impede such efforts. Faculty members may differ, however, in terms of how their world-views or religious faith informs their scholarship.

In many ways Diekema's definition does not differ in too great a way from the definitions discussed later in this chapter offered by the American Association of University Professors (AAUP). The difference between what Diekema proposes and what the AAUP has historically proposed pertains to his institutional or corporate understanding of academic freedom. Diekema defines corporate "academic freedom [as] the foundational principle granted only to academic institutions (colleges and universities) and designed to protect their corporate autonomy; that is their freedom from interference by external forces in the affairs of the institution" (2000, p. 86). Diekema claims that institutions, as the environments where faculty members generate and disseminate knowledge, have a responsibility to be free from forces that may seek to impede such efforts. But institutions like individuals may also differ in terms of how their particular worldview influences the scholarship being generated by members in their respective communities. In the same sense the practice of academic freedom may look different between a campus such as Notre Dame and a campus such as BYU. In essence, Catholicism and Mormonism yield different understandings of metaphysics and thus different ethical practices in areas such as academic freedom.

Anthony Diekema is not alone in attempting to define the nature of the relationship shared by faith-informed scholarship and academic freedom. Treatments of this issue abound (see, for example, Easton, 1957; Ericson, 1991; Habecker, 1991; Hoekema, 1996; Kliever, 1988; Litfin, 2004; Logan, 1991; May, 1988; McConnell, 1993; Moots and Gaffney, 1979; Nuechterlein, 1993; Wagner, 2006; Williams, 1953; Zagano, 1990). On many church-related college campuses, statements of faith to which faculty members are asked to ascribe are viewed as expressions of what Diekema identifies as institutional or corporate academic freedom. As a result, Eugene B. Habecker claims, "academic freedom must be subordinate to the overarching mission of the organization" (1991, p. 177). In contrast, Kenneth Wagner argues that statements of faith are "a troubling constraint that many of these [church-related] schools impose on their faculty" (2006, p. 21). Nussbaum also struggles with such statements for similar reasons.

Part of what divides scholars such as Habecker and Wagner is the definition of academic freedom as it stands in relation to larger metaphysical definitions of humanity. In *The Nature and Destiny of Man* (the Gifford Lectures given between 1938 and 1940), Reinhold Niebuhr contended that humanity proved to be a problem unto itself but that a distinction existed between what he identified as the classical view, the Christian view, and the modern view. For Niebuhr, the "classical man" as embodied by Greek tragedy viewed life as being at war with itself. As a result, "there is no solution, or only a tragic solution for the conflict between the vitalities of life and the principle of measure. Zeus remains God. But one is prompted to both admiration and pity to those who defy him" (1941, p. 11). For Niebuhr, the Christian "man is, according to the Biblical view, a created and finite existence in both body and spirit" (1941, p. 12). His or her full identity and freedom, however, depend on God. Absent God's grace, human beings are also at odds with themselves as a result of their sinful nature. Niebuhr's "modern man" is not at odds with himself but at times with the larger world. Humanity is now free from sin and set on a course of greater and greater forms of social and moral progress.

Despite the indebtedness that the modern understanding of humanity faces in relation to the Christian understanding, we propose that individual and communal forms of academic freedom are defined in relation to at least two of the three metaphysical constructs detailed by Niebuhr—the modern and the Christian. An understanding of academic freedom that emanates from a modern view of humanity focuses more on the generation and dissemination of truth apart from forces that might seek to suppress or even oppress such efforts. In contrast, an understanding of academic freedom that emanates from a Christian view of humanity focuses more on the generation and dissemination of truth yielded in the light of God's grace. When it comes to the relationship shared by faith-informed scholarship and academic freedom, differences concerning academic freedom are most intricately seen first and foremost at the level of metaphysics and then at the level of a moral practice such as academic freedom. For better or worse, differences in definition concerning academic freedom are at times more about human nature than about academic freedom.

A Brief Comparative History of Faith-Informed Scholarship and Academic Freedom

The fact that different understandings of academic freedom are often about human nature can be observed by studying historical narratives about academic freedom. Historiographical commitments make a difference. In particular, whether such commitments stem from a modern or a Christian understanding of humanity, one will likely see the development of the practice of academic freedom in the United States in one of two ways. On one hand, a modern understanding may propel historians to see the development of academic freedom as an effort to gain autonomy from various forces. On the other hand, a Christian understanding of humanity may lead historians to see the development of academic freedom as an effort to enrich the way truth is yielded in light of God's grace.

Perhaps the most noted historians of academic freedom are Richard Hofstadter and Walter P. Metzger. In *The Development of Academic Freedom in the United States* (1955), Hofstadter and Metzger offer a comprehensive history of this practice. In many ways the evaluative framework against which they trace the development of academic freedom assumes the ideals of the modern concept of humanity (thus the change is progressive and not regressive). In the first portion of their book, Hofstadter discusses academic freedom as it developed in the universities of Europe and how it eventually found its way to the colleges of the United States. In the second portion of the book, Metzger discusses academic freedom as it developed in what became a uniquely American understanding of the research university. Although they intend to provide a history of academic freedom in the United States, Hofstadter and Metzger spend only seventy-seven out of five hundred six pages addressing the origins of this practice before establishment of Harvard College in 1636. In their joint assessment, "Part One deals with an age overshadowed by religious and theological questions, Part Two with an age preoccupied with science and social problems" (pp. x–xi).

In their opinion "the university, not the college, became the model institution" (1955, p. xii). This model institution did not appear at one particular time, but the key date in terms of its origins in the United States is approximately 1865.

The Civil War had come to a close, and students who had traveled to Germany to earn advanced degrees began to climb to positions of influence in the American academy. At the close of his portion of this history, Hofstadter claims that during the pre–Civil War period, "the academic man was only beginning to be really professional" (p. 262). This professional understanding of the academic life was embodied by the scholars who populated the German academy. According to Metzger, "When the German professor spoke of academic freedom, he referred to a condition summed up by two words: *Lernfreiheit* and *Lehrfreiheit*" (p. 386). *Lernfreiheit* referred more to the absence of administrative regulations in relation to the education of students. As an attempt to free their minds for scholarly pursuits, students were deemed free to live wherever and study whatever, provided they passed the exam awaiting them at the end of their course of study. *Lehrfreiheit* referred to the "freedom of teaching and freedom of inquiry" offered to professors (p. 387). As a result, academic freedom, as the Germans defined it, was not simply the right of professors to speak without fear or favor but also the atmosphere of consent that surrounded the whole process of research and instruction" (p. 387).

Although the German notions of *Lernfreiheit* and *Lehrfreiheit* found their way into the academic culture in the United States in less than complete forms, their influence eventually became part of the impetus behind the formation of the AAUP in 1915. According to Metzger, "The first attempt of the AAUP to work out the scope and limits of academic freedom was Committee A's Report on Academic Freedom and Academic Tenure of 1915 (1955, p. 481). The initial report of this committee filed in 1915 found that "academic freedom was the end: due process, tenure, and establishment of professional competence were regarded as the necessary means" (p. 481). This sentiment was formalized in 1940 with the adoption of the Statement of Principles on Academic Freedom. Metzger concluded that the acceptance of this statement codified the nature and the place of academic freedom in American higher education.

The only reference to religion in the report the AAUP adopted in 1940 is one stating that any limitations on the exercise of academic freedom as a result of "religious commitments or other aims of the institution should be clearly stated in writing at the time of the appointment" (http://www.aaup.org/AAUP/pubsres/policydocs/1940statement.htm). Although this statement says little about religious commitments in relation to the practice of academic freedom, one can fairly assume that this singular reference identifies such commitments on the part of an institution as a hindrance more than an aid. At the outset of their text, however, Hofstadter and Metzger both offer that no one reading it should detect an "aggressive secularism" (p. xii) merely because "religious leaders figure in an exceptionally prominent way among the opponents of intellectual freedom in the first half of our story"—the period leading up to the influence of the German academy and the codification of the statement adopted in 1940 by the AAUP (pp. xi–xii). Nonetheless, Hoftstadter and Metzger give that impression that religious institutions remain unenlightened about true religious freedom. In relation to the statement adopted in 1940 by the AAUP, Metzger acknowledges, "When an institution was ready to be enlightened [about the practice of academic freedom], it had a formula and a text to draw upon" (1955, p. 490).

Although Hofstadter and Metzger may tell the most widely noted story concerning the development of academic freedom in the United States, their story of progression and enlightenment is not the only one. In contrast to Hofstadter and Metzger's historiography, William J. Hoye and George M. Marsden's historiography draws on a Christian concept of humanity. Hofstadter and Metzger see the past generation of religious leaders as being "culpable for their indifference or opposition to academic freedom" (p. xii). Neither Hoye nor Marsden shares that view. The issue is not that various leaders have in fact needlessly oppressed scholarly efforts at times in the name of religious belief. Scholars who possess both a Christian concept of humanity (Noll, 1994) and a modern concept of humanity (White, 1955) confirm such details. The issue is that perhaps academic freedom has a history that predates *Lehrfreiheit* and *Lernfreiheit*.

In his article entitled "The Religious Roots of Academic Freedom," Hoye contends that "academic freedom is one of those cultural values shaped, or at least influenced, by the Christian religion" (1997, p. 409). Hoye goes on to argue that "it is not totally by chance that the first known mention of academic freedom in Western history occurs in an official document of a pope" (p. 414). The issue at stake for Pope Honorius III in the 1200s was that the University of Bologna was being pressured by local officials to require students to pledge their allegiance to the city. Academic freedom was not viewed to be a privilege automatically bestowed on members of a given community. In fact, Bologna officials claimed only an entity such as the state could bestow such a privilege. In contrast, Pope Honorius III "presupposed its existence and value as being grounded in the very nature of academic life, arising from within and not from without" (p. 415).

With the medieval university in mind, Hoye claims that "both the idea of the university and the idea of academic freedom can be called gifts of medieval Christianity to the modern world, albeit in a secularized form" (1997, p. 415). To gain further verification of such a claim, one needs to look no farther than the origins of the word *university*. This word is identified with the intention of such an institution to reach across barriers offered not only by academic disciplines but also by nationalities. Hoye notes that in the medieval university one finds scholars such as Thomas Aquinas (Italy), who studied in Cologne and Paris and then taught in Paris. A second example, John Duns Scotus (Scotland), studied and taught in both Paris and Oxford. For Thomas Aquinas, such freedom was necessary to pose the questions that he addresses in his *Summa Theologica* concerning the existence and nature of God.

Like Hoye, George Marsden acknowledges that one must look to sources such as the medieval university for a complete history of academic freedom. In particular, he argues, "One of the oldest meanings of 'academic freedom' is that educational institutions should be able to set their own standards, free from undue outside interference" (1998, p. 14). In the American context, the towering influence of the 1940 statement makes an appreciation for sources such as the medieval university improbable. Regardless, such an appreciation is necessary if one is to see the 1940 statement and the subsequent commentary issued by the AAUP as being problematic in relation to matters of religious faith and scholarship. Marsden points out that the 1940 statement "implied that religious discrimination in hiring was a departure from a higher standard that would remove religion as a factor in choosing faculty" (p. 12). He also acknowledges that the interpretive commentary issued by the AAUP in 1970 makes "explicit that any departure from the norm of freedom from religious tests was undesirable" (p. 12).

Marsden in no way seeks to tell the story of academic freedom in relation to the efforts of the AAUP as a way of dispelling the significance of such a practice. In fact, he contends that "scholars should be as free as is possible within the framework of their other higher commitments to explore and communicate even unpopular and unconventional ideas" (1993, pp. 232–233). In actuality, the point of Marsden's account of academic freedom is to draw attention to the larger notion that "academic freedom as it was originally defined in the United States assumed a universal science that required only open-minded free inquiry to flourish" (p. 233). Although such a definition relates well to the modern concept of humanity, it relates unfavorably with the Christian concept of humanity and perhaps an emerging postmodern or postliberal concept of humanity that even Reinhold Niebuhr never envisioned. For Marsden, "Given the widespread recognition today that all science operates within boundaries of precommitments shaped by interpretive traditions [such as the modern concept of humanity] it may be time for a major reexamination of the assumptions concerning academic freedom and religion" (p. 232).

Although uncertainty abounds about the future of postmodernity and perhaps even a postmodern concept of humanity, society is unlikely to initiate a retreat into modernity and its accompanying concept of humanity. As a result, the story of academic freedom and the underlying assumptions inherent in both the AAUP's 1940 statement and subsequent forms of interpretive commentary prove not to be the only story or the end of the story. Perhaps even the AAUP itself is beginning to recognize this shift. An AAUP-appointed subcommittee revisited the issue of academic freedom in 1988 and 1996. In 1996, this subcommittee offered that the AAUP should not prosecute cases concerning academic freedom that originate with institutions "that persist in retaining religious tests for faculty, so long as they are entirely up front about their standards and follow due process" (Marsden, 1998, p. 12).

Overall, the difference between the histories of academic freedom provided by Hofstadter and Metzger and later Hoye and Marsden are telling in relation to how concepts of humanity influence perceptions of academic freedom in the academy. Such a tension is not simply part of the history of the academy, however, but part of how individual scholars are trying currently to think through the relationship shared by religious faith–informed scholarship and academic freedom.

Comparing Individual Perspectives of Faith-Informed Scholarship and Academic Freedom

If the telling of the history of academic freedom reflects the differences acknowledged by Reinhold Niebuhr in terms of his modern concept of humanity and his Christian concept of humanity, one is probably not surprised to find that the perspectives of individual scholars are also divided along similar lines. Scholars such as Richard Rorty provide a voice for academic freedom reflective of a modern concept of humanity, and scholars such as William Cavanaugh provide a voice for academic freedom reflective of a Christian concept of humanity. New voices such as Stanley Fish, however, take an approach to academic freedom reflective of a postliberal concept of humanity.

Richard Rorty is arguably the most influential American philosopher of our generation. In many ways, he may prove to be the heir apparent to John Dewey in a postmodern key. Dewey in his time served as the founding president of the AAUP. Ironically, Rorty may have inherited not only much of Dewey's spirit of pragmatism but also his voice in relation to matters such as academic freedom. Despite other postmodern commitments, Rorty, like Dewey, reflects a concept of modern humanity whose freedom and individuation are in process. Educational institutions exist to instill in students hope that personal freedom comes with progressing forms of democracy. As a result, Rorty contends that "the point of non-vocational higher education is . . . to help students realize that they can reshape themselves—that they can rework the self-image foisted on them by their past, the self-image that makes them competent citizens, into a new self-image, one that they themselves have to create" (1999, p. 114). In essence, primary and secondary education is a process of socialization—a process by which students become familiar with their elders and their viewpoints. In contrast, higher education is a process of individualization—a process by which students become familiar with themselves. Both processes exist in the larger arena of a progressive and thus hopeful democracy.

As a result, Rorty views the practice of academic freedom as an essential part of the socialization process. Perhaps Rorty's view on this practice is most reflective of a modern concept of humanity at the point where he argues that academic freedom "is a matter that has to be left up to individual college teachers to do or not do as they think fit, as their sense of responsibility to their students and their society inspires them" (1999, p. 123). For Rorty, "the success of the . . . AAUP in enforcing academic freedom means that college teachers set their own agendas" (p. 116). One point that needs to be clarified is that Rorty does not believe that freedom and the larger arena of democracy exist beyond us in some Platonic ideal. His understanding of academic freedom is one informed by the belief that "the social function of American colleges is to help students see that the national narrative around which their socialization has centered is an open-ended one" (p. 124). Students need to work with professors who exhibit an appreciation for this narrative by seeking to advance it. As a result, Rorty claims, "The only point in having real live professors around instead of just computer terminals, videotapes and mimeoed lecture notes is that students need to have freedom enacted before their eyes by actual human beings" (p. 125).

Although Rorty's view concerning the practice of academic freedom emerges from a modern view of humanity, William T. Cavanaugh's view arises from a Christian concept. Cavanaugh has spent the majority of his career to date studying what he has called "political theology." In other words, Cavanaugh is interested in how the church might inform one's political identity and practices versus, for example, the democratic state to which both Rorty and Dewey refer. Some institutions of higher education may view themselves as entities that inherit their primary sense of identity from the church and not the state. Regardless of a particular institution's locus of identity, Cavanaugh argues "that the prevailing understanding of academic freedom is seriously deficient, both in its focus on the individual professor and in its understanding of freedom" (2004, p. 31). In fact, he argues that institutions that derive their identity from the church "can foster a fuller practice of academic freedom" than institutions that derive their identity from the state (p. 31).

Drawing on the distinction Isaiah Berlin made between positive and negative freedom, Cavanaugh contends that the practice of academic freedom as defined by the AAUP (and perhaps also scholars such as Rorty) is reflective of negative freedom or the absence of restraint. In contrast, Cavanaugh claims that the practice of academic freedom he will offer is one reflective of positive freedom or "the ability to achieve some good purpose"—a view that echoes Niebuhr's understanding of the Christian concept of humanity. The ability of positive freedom to achieve its end or purpose is driven by its willingness to inherit certain limiting conditions. For Cavanaugh, institutions that derive their identity from the church view such conditions as orthodoxy and authority. In orthodoxy, the community and those individuals who participate in it are bound by a common worldview that is theologically informed. This worldview in turn becomes the basis for authority in the community. As a result of this view of authority, Cavanaugh would likely agree with Rorty's assertion "that the typical administrator would not dream of trying to interfere with a teacher's attempt to carry out such responsibilities" (1999, p. 123). Where they differ (beyond their view of freedom), however, is that Cavanaugh views academic freedom as a communal practice whereas Rorty views it as an individual practice. In essence, Cavanaugh contends that "there is no prima facie reason to suppose that the university itself cannot be the subject of academic freedom" (2004, p. 38).

On the surface, Rorty's and Cavanaugh's viewpoints appear to be extremes on some dialectical plane concerning the practice of academic freedom. By adding Stanley Fish's viewpoint concerning this practice to the conversation, however, we offer that such differences are more subtle yet also more penetrating. Fish works primarily in the area of literary theory, but he also served as an administrator. In one sense, Fish's perspective likely pushes us to think about what may come next on Niebuhr's typology regarding various concepts of humanity. One may wonder whether a postmodern or a postliberal concept is now deemed necessary. In another sense, perhaps Fish's perspective echoes a classical view of humanity. His views at times remind us of Niebuhr's contention that the classical concept of humanity is one that finds "no solution, or only a tragic solution for the conflict between the vitalities of life and the principle of measure" (1941, p. 11). Ironically, Cavanaugh would likely agree with Fish's assertion that our ability to affirm various forms of freedom of expression are "dependent for their force on an exception that literally carves out the space in which expression can then emerge" (1994, p. 103). As a result,

Fish contends, "without restriction, without an inbuilt sense of what would be meaningless to say or not say, there could be no assertion and no reason for asserting it" (p. 103).

Rorty would likely reject such an assertion concerning the need for restriction. In contrast, Cavanaugh would likely affirm it and contend that such an assertion is an expression of the necessary role of orthodoxy and authority. In essence, both Fish and Cavanaugh recognize that our ability to make meaning as human beings is contingent on the communities with which we identify ourselves. Fish is less specific than Cavanaugh on this point. Cavanaugh clearly identifies the church as the interpretive community he has in mind. Fish leaves one to wonder how such interpretive communities might be defined. Regardless of their similarities, their differences quickly come to the surface. For Fish, "it is immoral for academics or for academic institutions to proclaim moral views" (2003, n.p.). In particular, he contends that "the unfettered expression of ideas is a cornerstone of liberal democracy; it is a prime political value. It is not however, an academic value, and if we come to regard it as our primary responsibility, we will default on the responsibilities assigned to us and come to be what no one pays us to be—political agents" (2003, n.p.). Cavanaugh would contend that the authority of orthodoxy forges a political identity. One cannot accept such a worldview and not see scholarship as an expression of love of God and love of neighbor. As one who views academic freedom in the light of progressing forms of democracy, Rorty likely would also disagree with Fish on this point, as scholarship is a means of advancing such a cause.

Institutional Examples of Faith-Informed Scholarship and Academic Freedom

If Cavanaugh is correct, the greater the institutional awareness of the theological tradition or narrative that informs its identity, the greater is the ability of members to freely practice what past generations of theologians would identify as "faith seeking understanding." Administrators in such institutions possess the right and the responsibility to exert authority through the decisions they are charged with making. The source of their authority, however, is not found in the office they hold but in the tradition they are charged with advancing.

To provide concrete examples of how such authority has been exercised in religious institutions, we now turn our attention to two institutional examples—one is Catholic (the Catholic University of America) and one is Protestant (Calvin College). These examples are not offered as an attempt to indicate whether these institutions properly or improperly respect the practice of academic freedom: we offer them as examples of institutions striving to be places that sort through the complexities that invariably emerge when a genuine relationship is attempting to be struck between religious faith and scholarship. One cannot deny that both the efforts of the scholars in question and the processes by which their work was evaluated are reflective of what Niebuhr identified as a Christian understanding of humanity.

Perhaps the most widely publicized situation in recent history concerning the exercise of authority in relation to matters of religious faith-informed scholarship and academic freedom took place at the Catholic University of America (CUA) during the latter half of the twentieth century (Cramer, 1986; Curran, 1980, 1987, 1990, 1992; Kurland, 1986; Walton, 1990; Witham, 1991). This situation surfaced as a result of competing theological conclusions. Compounding this situation are two particular historical qualities that make CUA distinctive in American higher education. First, unlike all other Catholic colleges and universities in the United States, CUA was initially established in 1887 to serve as a center for graduate education. As a result, original research has proved to be at the heart of the university's mission from its earliest days. And unlike all other Catholic colleges and universities in the United States, CUA was established by the Vatican, Pope Leo XIII in particular. Although CUA currently refers to itself as a free and autonomous academic institution, it continues to share a special relationship with not only the Vatican but also with the United States Conference of Catholic Bishops. The difference in this relationship is that most Catholic colleges and universities share a special relationship with their founding religious order versus the Vatican and the bishops.

The particular situation of interest at CUA revolved around Father Charles E. Curran, who served on the university's theology faculty. Father Curran's area of expertise was moral theology. He had proved to be quite influential in relation to matters involving the nature of human life, sexuality, and the sacrament of marriage. In one sense, his views on such topics were seen as attempts to expand the teachings of the Catholic Church. In another sense, his views on such topics were seen as affronts to such teachings. Father Curran's views came into conflict with the views of Pope Paul VI's teaching in the encyclical entitled *Humanae Vitae* (issued July 29, 1968), which essentially denounced the use of artificial contraception. In contrast, Father Curran "insisted that the basic teaching condemning artificial contraception for married couples was wrong and that a Roman Catholic could dissent in theory and in practice from such a teaching" (Curran, 1979, p. 43). He "personally [saw] no moral problem in using other forms of contraception as a means of exercising responsible parenthood" (Curran, 1982, p. 144). Although Curran's position concerning artificial contraception proved to be the occasion for such a difference, the underlying issue proved to be whether dissent in theory or practice was understood to be an acceptable exercise of the practice of academic freedom at CUA.

Controversy surrounding Father Curran and his views began as early as the 1960s. In 1967, his colleagues recommended to CUA's governing board that Father Curran be promoted and given tenure, but "the governing board, then composed entirely of bishops, . . . rejected the recommendation, expressing displeasure with his [Curran's] liberal views" (Kurland, 1986, p. 43). In this instance, the board rescinded its decision four days later and granted Curran tenure. Controversy concerning his views continued to follow Curran throughout his career at CUA. On August 18, 1986, Archbishop James A. Hickey, the chancellor of CUA, informed Curran that the prefect of the Congregation for the Doctrine of Faith, Cardinal Joseph Ratzinger (now Pope Bendeict XVI), had informed him that Curran was no longer eligible to serve as a professor of Catholic theology. The investigation leading up to such a decision was initiated in 1979. On June 2, 1988, the governing board of CUA accepted the decision of the Vatican through the Congregation for the Doctrine of Faith. The Vatican and the governing board of CUA had determined that a professor of Catholic theology could not issue dissent in relation to encyclical teachings.

A less widely publicized situation concerning the exercise of authority in relation to matters of religious faith-informed scholarship and academic freedom took place at Calvin College. Founded in 1876, Calvin is a liberal arts college that embodies the Reformed tradition of Protestant Christianity. In particular, Calvin is a college of the Christian Reformed Church that has its roots in the theology of the college's namesake, John Calvin. In contrast to the situation at CUA, which involved differing views concerning matters of theology, this particular situation of interest at Calvin involved differing views concerning matters of theology and science. The differences are not necessarily drawn clearly along lines separating science and theology. In fact, what is really at stake in this situation is how religious faith and scholarship should in fact be integrated. Ironically, perhaps part of the reason this situation was less widely publicized concerning the exercise of authority in relation to matters of faith-informed scholarship and academic freedom than at CUA was that the situation at Calvin may more aptly be described as a nonexercise of authority.

The particular situation of interest involved the publication in 1986 of Howard J. Van Till's book, *The Fourth Day: What the Bible and the Heavens Are Telling Us about the Creation.* Van Till served as a professor of physics at Calvin until 1997. Over the course of his career, he conducted research in areas such as condensed-matter physics and astronomy. He may be most well known, however, for his work concerning the nature of the relationship shared by the traditional boundaries of his discipline and his faith. Although *The Fourth Day* proved to be his most comprehensive treatment of this particular area of inquiry, it also proved to be his most controversial. The majority of Van Till's text includes quite complex refutations of both naturalistic evolutionism and special creationism, and the concluding chapter includes his proposal of a theory that would transcend the dialectic forged by evolution and creation. Van Till refers to his theory as the "creationomic perspective." In simple terms, this theory "is achieved when natural science is placed in the framework of biblical theism" (1986, p. 250).

Several important voices in the Christian Reformed Church and beyond began to contend that Van Till's proposition proved to be too great an accommodation to evolution and thus compromised the integrity of the Biblical narrative of creation. Anthony J. Diekema was serving as president of Calvin College at the time *The Fourth Day* was published and recounts the events of this controversy in his work on academic freedom. According to Diekema, the due process measures concerning academic freedom "were set in motion and, because some of the allegations focused on ecclesiastical and creedal matters, a special five-member study committee of the board of trustees was established to assess the legitimacy of those issues" (2000, p. 29). After a year of examining this situation, this committee recommended to the full board that the calls for Van Till's dismissal be rejected. The Christian Reformed Church soon launched its own inquiry, however. In 1991, the church issued its own report and supported Van Till's exercise of academic freedom and Calvin College's decisions in relation to this matter. Diekema noted that in 1999 Van Till's scholarly efforts eventually even earned him the Faith and Learning Award from the Calvin College Alumni Association.

Overall, the issue at stake in both these stories is how larger theological narratives or traditions inform the practice of academic freedom in human communities. Although they came to different conclusions about how to act, administrators at CUA and at Calvin drew on the Catholic and the Reformed traditions, respectively. The administration at CUA chose to act; the administration at Calvin chose not to. In both cases, religious faith not only informed the scholarly practices of Charles Curran and Howard Van Till but also the concept and practice of academic freedom.

As this chapter reveals, a robust understanding of the practice of academic freedom can be held intact in environments where religious faith informs the nature of scholarship. The real issue is not whether disciplines such as science and religion stand in opposition to one another but whether one is conscious of the larger metaphysical considerations that inform the practice of academic freedom. Reinhold Niebuhr's distinction between the Christian concept of humanity and the modern concept of humanity is but one way to bring such considerations to light. Regardless, one must recognize that the practice of academic freedom is not stagnant. In fact, it possesses a history, and that history has changed over time. Martha Nussbaum's assertion concerning the differences found on the Notre Dame campus and the BYU campus may prove to be fair on the surface. But by dismissing the significance of metaphysics in relation to such matters, she creates the illusion that the practice of academic freedom possesses both a singular history and a singular definition. As we have seen in this chapter, differing concepts of humanity drive differing understandings of the practice of academic freedom. In recent years, the modern concept of humanity has fueled a predominant understanding, but the Christian concept of humanity has fueled an understanding with a longer history. In fact, such a history may be what has propelled scholars such as Gavin D'Costa to contend that in institutions that recognize such a history, "there is no clear case that academic freedom is called into question. Rather, the opposite may occur: genuine creativity and interdisciplinary research may occur in universities accountable to a unified vision of life, grace, and love" (2005, p. xi).

Faith-Informed Scholarship and the Larger Tournament of Narratives

O NE SHOULD EXPECT EDUCATION to serve religious ends argues Neal Postman in his book *The End of Education* (1995). The reason, he claims, is that for education to make sense, it "must have a god to serve, or, even better, several gods" (p. 4). By "god" or "gods," Postman does not mean the Christian, Jewish, or Muslim God or the Hindu pantheon of transcendent beings. Instead, he uses the word *god* to refer to a narrative "that tells of origins and envisions a future, a story that constructs ideals, prescribes rules of conduct, provides a source of authority, and, above all, gives a sense of continuity and purpose" (pp. 5–6).

During the past century, the god or narrative that guided scholarship in higher education remained the scientific story. Yet in *The Postmodern Condition: A Report on Knowledge,* Jean-François Lyotard (1984) observes the contradiction of which scholars began to be aware regarding the nature of modern science. Although science usually judges the majority of narratives as fables, when science moves from seeking useful regularities to the truth, "it is obliged to legitimate the rules of its own game" (p. xxiii). Such forms of legitimation written by scientists not surprisingly have taken the form of "some grand narrative, such as the dialectics of Spirit, the hermeneutics of meaning, the emancipation of the rational or working subject, or the creation of wealth" (p. xxiii). The dominant Enlightenment narrative that informed science was that "the rule of consensus between the sender and addressee of a statement with truth-value is deemed acceptable if it is cast in terms of a possible unanimity between rational minds" (p. xxiii). Because science and scientists have proved incapable of convincingly justifying any of these narratives, Lyotard claimed we moved beyond the modern period to the postmodern, which is defined by "incredulity toward metanarratives" (p. xxiv).

Ironically, despite the supposed incredulity in the postmodern university toward metanarratives, the appeal to various scientific or religious metanarratives has not decreased. In fact, Lyotard, like Nietzsche before him, may have offered a false prophecy about the postmodern condition. Instead, something similar to Samuel Huntington's thesis (1996) about *The Clash of Civilizations and the Remaking of World Order* may be more at play in the academy; however, instead of a clash of civilizations, the postmodern condition in the academy has produced, to borrow James McClendon's term, "a tournament of narratives" (1986, p. 143).

Although secular voices and perspectives continue to dominate the academic tournament and one still finds triumphal prophetic stories or predictions about what the death of God will do for society and scholarship (Dawkins, 2006), one now also finds prominent scholars producing their own narratives about the contemporary university that reverse the tables on Nietzsche. They claim not only that God is not dead but also that the secular university needs God (or at least religion) or it could die. At the very least, it might lose (or perhaps has already lost) its soul (see, for example, Lewis's *Excellence Without a Soul: How a Great University Forgot Education,* 2006).

The first part of this chapter offers an overview of the critical narratives told by religious scholars about what they variously call the "modern," "liberal," or "secular" university. We have chosen narratives from Catholic, Lutheran, mainline Protestant, Reformed, and evangelical scholars who tell quite similar stories about the modern research university and modern approaches to scholarship but with slightly different types of emphasis. What their stories entail for the future of faith-informed scholarship and faith-based universities is also subject to a variety of interpretations. Nonetheless, many authors believe that the problems with secularized universities point to the need and open the way for religion to make a vital contribution to scholarship, university life, and a larger vision of the academy. The second part of this chapter discusses what these scholars say will or should be the place of religiously informed scholarship in the postmodern and postsecular academy.

Expounders of Decline or Decay in the Academy

Stories about the decline or decay of particular aspects of higher education are not new in the history of higher education (see, for example, Reuben, 1996; Sloan, 1994). Nonetheless, the commonalities of contemporary declension stories often say something about the future direction of higher education and some of its problems. The following paragraphs review five such narratives that pertain directly to the future role of religion and faith-informed scholarship in the academy.

Alasdair MacIntyre on the Irrationality and Fragmentation of the Liberal University

One of the early critiques of the university's exclusion of religion came from Alasdair MacIntyre in the last chapter of his book, *Three Rival Versions of Moral Enquiry: Encyclopedia, Genealogy and Tradition* (1990). MacIntyre tells the story of the growing inability of the liberal university to justify itself. In previous chapters MacIntyre described and chronicled the failure of the encyclopedic vision of the liberal university. This vision, as embodied in the *Encyclopedia Britannica,* saw the university as seeking to embody "a unified secular vision of the world and of the place of knowledge and enquiry within it" (p. 216).

The hope for a unified universal system of knowledge and an educated public that would embrace such a project, MacIntyre claims, eventually became undermined by three trends. First, inquiry become so fragmented and specialized that scholars could not find a place for their results in a larger unified vision of knowledge. Old metaphors envisioning knowledge as a tree (René Descartes) or a house (Jacques Barzun) disappeared. Second, the educated public by which such a vision must be sustained began to disintegrate. By educated public MacIntyre does not mean those with a certain level of education but those that share "common fundamental assumptions the basis of which it is able to articulate disagreements and organize debates, [those that read] to a significant degree the same texts, [draw] upon the same figures of speech, and [share] standards of victory and defeat in intellectual debate"; moreover, the educated public carries on these practices "in and through institutional means, clubs and societies, periodicals, and more formal education institutions" (pp. 216–217). Third, moral and theological truth were no longer acknowledged as objects of substantive inquiry but were instead marginalized to the realm of privatized belief.

MacIntyre argues that this last development meant that the sources for the framework that originally provided the unity of knowledge were largely expelled from the academic arena (see also Reuben, 1996). To dissolve antagonism and emasculate hostility, the university had to respond by removing the ideal of the unity of truth. This move, MacIntyre argues, began to make universities culturally irrelevant. This irrelevance is now being pointed out, MacIntyre suggests, by forces outside academia who are questioning its purpose and function. According to MacIntyre, "the official spokespersons for the academic status quo have with rare exceptions responded with stunning ineptitudes" to this external questioning. The reason, he claims, is that the contemporary university "lacks the resources to answer" (p. 221).

The proper answer, MacIntyre says, is to acknowledge that "universities are places where conceptions of and standards of rational justification are elaborated, put to work in the detailed practices of enquiry, and themselves rationally evaluated, so that only from the university can the wider society learn how to conduct its own debates, practical or theoretical, in a rationally defensible way" (p. 222). The contemporary university, however, does not fulfill this purpose because it has not allowed diverse concepts and standards of rational justification to be developed, tested, and debated.

The reason is that the liberal university made a mistake when it sought to correct features of premodern universities and colleges. These institutions enforced agreement on standards of rationality and excluded points of view too much at odds with the underpinnings of rational inquiry. The liberal university sought to correct the injustices under this system, but when undertaking this correction it mistakenly believed "human rationality is such and the methods and procedures which it has devised and in which it has embodied itself are such that, if freed from external constraints and most notably from the constraints imposed by religious and moral tests, it will produce not only progress in enquiry but also agreement among all rational persons as to what the rationally justified conclusions of such enquiry are" (p. 225). Earlier in

Whose Justice? Which Rationality? (1988), MacIntyre convincingly argued that this claim proved false. Because this belief proved false, it has resulted in increasing disarray, especially in areas outside science where policies of enforced exclusion no longer exist and where agreement on technique and procedure substitutes for agreement on substance. In disciplines such as literary interpretation, one finds "change of fashion rather than progress in enquiry" (1990, p. 225). In ethics and theology, which require a degree of resolution regarding fundamental disagreements so that rational inquiry may be advanced, the liberal university can provide no solutions. The increase in applied ethics courses, MacIntyre claims, actually supports his claim. Moral problems and differences are not rationally solved but merely understood. Neither theology nor moral philosophy is allowed or able to provide the principles of order for the curriculum they originally did. The curriculum is no longer a whole and can no longer be rationally justified as a whole. MacIntyre thus concludes: "And insofar as the university as an institution could only be justified by appeal to some specific rational understanding of how human goods are to be ordered and the place within that ordering of the goods of enquiry, the absence from the university of any form of rational enquiry providing such a systematic understanding of how goods are to be ordered inevitably deprives the university of any adequate response to its external critics" (p. 227). In the end, it means the modern liberal university can no longer rationally justify its existence to the wider public.

In another article MacIntyre (2006) deepens this critique by examining the general university culture. With the multiplication of disciplines has come increasing specialization. What it means for the education of students is that they receive specialized training in a major without considering or even knowing what they need to learn. Instead students learn bits and pieces of information and knowledge. The tragedy, MacIntyre writes, is "the question of how these bits and pieces might be related to one another, of whether they are or are not parts that contribute to some whole, of what, if anything, it all adds up to, not merely commonly goes unanswered, it almost always goes unasked" (p. 11). The problem stems from the fact that no one takes responsibility for giving students the big picture that connects the parts.

Mark Schwehn and the Corruption of the Academic Vocation

In *Exiles from Eden: Religion and the Academic Vocation in America* (1993), Mark Schwehn chronicles a slightly different and less dire story of decline, although it also foretells dire consequences if not reversed. While MacIntyre describes the inability of the liberal university to further rational inquiry in various disciplines and about the purposes and unity of the university as a whole, Schwehn makes a different argument about the ability of universities to fulfill their stated purposes. He argues that the structure of modern universities such as Harvard "militates against some of the very purposes that it occasionally espouses" such as helping students lead ethical, meaningful lives or become "mature, morally perceptive human beings" (p. 9). In other words, we should not be surprised by the recent work decrying the loss of Harvard's soul (Lewis, 2006).

The problem, Schwehn argues, stems from the fact that of three concepts of the academic vocation—the cultivation of character, the transmission of knowledge and skills, and the making of knowledge—most academics in the modern research university understand their task as being the third in a way best represented by Max Weber's concept of academic work as primarily making knowledge. Rationality is a purely instrumental tool that aids the ultimate end of "mastery of the world."

Under this Weberian approach, character formation becomes understood as an activity separate from the transmission and making of knowledge. Schwehn notes, however, that this separation can only occur in two ways. First, the transmission of knowledge and skills must be construed as merely inculcation of information instead of "the development of a tradition of thought and learning" (p. 17). Echoing MacIntyre, he claims that most universities follow Weber in that they are no longer willing to transmit a particular tradition intentionally. When they reduce their activity to the transmission of information and training in skills, they no longer believe they need to shape "the moral substance or the habits of mind and action that determine character" (p. 17).

Second, the discovery of knowledge actually does encourage a particular kind of character formation or personality development. It produces "clarity, but not charity; honesty, but not friendliness; devotion to the calling, but not loyalty to particular and local communities of learning" (p. 18). These character qualities, however, are usually not considered virtues and do not necessarily lead to "mature, morally perceptive human beings" (p. 18).

Schwehn is quick to note that plenty of people in the academy still exhibit the virtues of humility, faith, self-sacrifice, and charity essential for the communal quest for knowledge and truth. He wonders, however, whether the secularization of the academy has perhaps undermined its ability to sustain those virtues and transmit them to the next generation. Schwehn believes sustaining these virtues requires certain religious vocabularies, practices, and affections that the secular university now lacks. In fact, the modern research university, by often focusing on the mastering of all things by calculation, has actually become the institutional sponsor of nihilistic and alienating approaches to life and thought. It ends up seeing humans as merely their own creators of meaning and knowledge instead of those who can seek, discover, and possess wisdom. In this situation, Schwehn maintains it "cannot credibly claim to be pursuing the life of virtue" (p. 135).

Douglas Sloan and the Limits of Modern Knowledge

Douglas Sloan tells a story of the modern university that has less to do with its deliberative or moral limits and more to do with the limits of its current methods of discovering knowledge. It is quite clear, however, that Sloan, similar to MacIntyre, believes these limits hamper the modern university from fulfilling its function in important ways. In his essay "Faith and Knowledge: Religion and the Modern University," Sloan outlines three problematic assumptions about knowing and knowable reality that dominated modern Western consciousness for most of the nineteenth and twentieth centuries. These assumptions, he notes, are so deeply ingrained that even when conscious of them "their influence remains strong, often determinative, for modern knowledge and experience" (2002, p. 4).

The first of these assumptions is that scholars can separate themselves from the object of study and that in fact the best way to know something is to "detach ourselves from it as much as possible and describe it as mere onlookers" (p. 4). The second assumption is that we can only discover agreed-upon knowledge through our physical senses. The third epistemological assumption is related in that it views all reality as inorganic, lifeless, and materialistic and therefore "is to be understood in terms of physical cause and effect, of external relationships, that is, mechanistically" (p. 5). It leads to a focus on quantitative ways of knowing that ignore the qualitative aspects of life.

These assumptions, Sloan points out, have had three important implications for our understanding of religion and knowledge. First, what religion understood as important—the realities of human-meaning value, purpose, truth, beauty, and goodness—are now often considered unknowable. Sloan concludes "under this way of knowing, the human being—no less than beings of the animal and plant kingdoms—is reduced to bare, material elements. And the moral and spiritual cannot be dealt with at all" (p. 6). Second, Sloan claims, the two-spheres approach to knowledge has resulted in reductionist models of humanity and nature. "Among the results are wrenching ethical, medical, ecological and cultural dilemmas, as the fullness of the human being is reduced to conformity with the less-than-human realities generated in the laboratory and then released upon a hapless public" (p. 6). Finally, it has given us the sharp split among faith, values, and meaning. Sloan, who clearly sees these three developments as problematic and believes many in the academy do so as well, is not hopeful about their ultimate rejection. Nonetheless, others make the argument that the larger culture outside the academy is starting to recognize the problems these ways of knowing entail.

George Marsden and the Demise of Progressive Scientific Humanism

George Marsden claims that the view of knowledge promoted by the academy in general could be called "progressive scientific humanism," which was an intellectual tradition represented by scholars such as John Dewey. According to this tradition, naturalistic science, using the methods Sloan outlined, would lead to progress in all areas of knowledge about which most people could agree. In this view, "sectarian religion would only get in the way of building this consensus necessary for a vital democratic society" (2002, p. 39). Today, however, the dream of progressive scientific humanism lies shattered. "For the first time in three centuries, the ideal that human progress will be achieved by ever-wider applications of scientific models to almost all of life seems passé. . . .

The promises of moral and intellectual consensus grounded on, or at least in harmony with, a naturalistic scientific outlook have just as surely collapsed. Progressive scientific humanism is another god that failed" (pp. 39–40).

The collapse of progressive scientific humanism has resulted in the university's inability to provide cultural leadership. Echoing MacIntyre's claims about the liberal university's failure to sustain a unified vision of knowledge, he argues that "the rest of the culture pays little attention to academia's cultural observers because academia's cultural observers have little that is coherent to say to it. Furthermore, because of its tenure system and residual scientific ideals, academia rewards the esoteric, the obscure, and the jargon-ridden" (p. 40). As a result, Marsden believes that the old ideal of the modern research university is no longer the standard by which to measure progress.

C. John Sommerville and the Decline of the Secular University

Echoes of Marsden's argument may also be found in C. John Sommerville's *The Decline of the Secular University* (2006). Sommerville makes clear at the beginning that his argument does not pertain to finances, enrollment numbers, or even cultural perceptions about the need for a degree from a secular university. "The American university is now bigger than ever, better funded, producing more of whatever it produces. Young people think they need a degree of some sort in order to participate in society fully" (pp. 7–8). The irony, Sommerville claims, is that despite all this power and prestige, "the secular university is increasingly marginal to American society" (p. 4). The reason underlying this irrelevance is that the secularism of universities has trivialized religion and therefore undermined the important role that religion plays in sustaining rational argument and particular types of conversation. The result is that the secular university now contains numerous weaknesses. It no longer gives attention to defining what is human, it seeks to maintain a dubious distinction between "facts" and "values," and it leads to universities' inability to understand the post–Cold War world where religion is vitally important. "The secularism that looked vital and self-sufficient in 1900 has exhausted itself before reaching its goals of offering wisdom and leadership to American life. By limiting the university's attention to what we supposedly could all agree on—the objective or rational—secularism has not fulfilled our hopes" (p. 121).

The ultimate result is that secularism has actually led to what he calls post-secularism, "a situation in which cultural fashion has replaced intellectual argument" (p. 6). Practically speaking, it means "universities are not really where we look for answers to our life questions" (p. 8). Secularity has precluded universities' being places where such questions are not merely asked but also pursued and, at times, answered. The tone of the debates surrounding universities is subsequently reduced to matters of financial accountability, a well-prepared workforce, and financially independent children with prospects of careers.

Summary of Narratives

Instead of stories of religion's demise, these authors claim that it is the contemporary secular narratives guiding the academy that are in some way limiting contemporary education and scholarship. Although they often use different names and terms, the narratives about the decline of particular types of universities (liberal, modern, secular) or particular movements dominant in universities (progressive scientific humanism, secularism) share a common language. These universities and movements are "imploding," "passé," "declining," "barren," "soulless," and "lacking virtue." MacIntyre and Sommerville complain that certain disciplines are ruled by cultural taste and fashion. At the heart of many of the diagnoses of sickness in secularism and secular universities is the difficulty such universities have in allowing the expression and promotion of diverse traditions of inquiry and thought about ultimate human questions and issues. The university, they argue, lacks a soul. It needs a different metanarrative to guide the story.

Narratives of Hope? The Postmodern, Postliberal, Postsecular University

Along with the narratives discussing the possible demise of the modern, secular university, these same scholars are also producing narratives of possible hope or at least suggestions for more hopeful directions when it comes to the postmodern and postsecular university. They believe the university of tomorrow needs religiously informed scholarship and religious universities for a variety of reasons. Some of the suggestions are rather modest, while others are quite grand and have even been described by their proponents as "utopian."

Alasdair MacIntyre: The Postliberal University

MacIntyre's solution to what he perceives as the failure of the liberal university is what he calls a "postliberal university." This university is "a place of constrained disagreement, of imposed participation in conflict, in which a central responsibility of higher education would be to initiate students into conflict" (1990, p. 231). Professors in this university would advance teaching and inquiry from a particular viewpoint while also fairly presenting and engaging rival viewpoints. Thus, in public lectures a professor would not pretend to speak to every reasonable person but would instead acknowledge commitment to some particular partisan standpoint. This approach would prove particularly helpful in advancing systematically conducted moral and theological inquiry where such agreement is required. Of course, professors would also need to play a role in ordering the conflicts and sustaining institutionalized forums for such conflicts to occur.

MacIntyre realizes that in such a pluralistic setting, what will occur is that different interpretive traditions would create rival universities, "each advancing its own enquiries in its own terms and each securing the type of agreement necessary to ensure the progress and flourishing of its enquires by its own set of exclusions and prohibitions, formal and informal" (1990, p. 234). Forums would also then be needed where rival universities could engage in debate, especially about the moral and theological underpinnings of their views. Oddly, Macintyre calls his vision "utopian." Others we will discuss who share a similar vision believe it is quite realistic and that the current American system currently functions in this manner.

What it practically means for Catholic universities, MacIntyre argues, is that they have a special calling. The role of a Catholic university, he believes, should be "to challenge its secular counterparts by recovering both for them and for itself a less fragmented conception of what an education beyond high school should be . . . " (2006, p. 10). MacIntyre proposes that Catholic universities formulate a three-year liberal arts curriculum that not only teaches specific knowledge from particular disciplines but also confronts questions not asked in specific disciplines. For example, "Is physics the fundamental discipline, so that everything else, including not only plant and nonhuman animal life, but also human actions and passions, is reducible to or determined by or explicable in terms of the fundamental laws of physics? Or is it instead the case that living organisms have properties that cannot be so explained that human beings transcend the limitations of other living organisms, so that their thought-informed actions are directed towards ends of which no naturalistic account can be given?" (p. 12). For MacIntyre, only a unified Catholic university with a faculty trained to explore broad questions across disciplines can help us address such questions.

Mark Schwehn: Help for Restoring the Academic Vocation

Like MacIntyre, Schwehn believes that a solution to what ails the contemporary academic vocation, and thus the modern academy, must involve recognition of what was lost from the original religiously inspired and informed universities. Schwehn believes, though, that the solution has less to do with initiating students into conflict and more with reappropriating the religious language, affections, and practices needed to sustain certain religious virtues. "The practice of certain spiritual virtues is and has always been essential to the process of learning, even within the secular academy" (1993, p. 41). The virtues he has in mind are those such as humility, faith, self-sacrifice, and charity that originated from a Christian context (but any person can acquire). Schwehn argues that such virtues are indispensable for learning in the academy.

Restoring religious piety to the academic vocation would redirect its moral direction and content. "For Weber, the point of academic life was *making* knowledge; under the present reconception, it is *seeking* the truth of matters. Instead of Weberian *mastery* of the world through calculation and control, academics ought primarily to seek understanding of the world through communal inquiry" (1993, p. 58). In this academy, teaching once again becomes the primary activity by which other activities are to be understood, interpreted, and evaluated. The virtues necessary for such teaching must then be cultivated, especially charity and friendship.

Douglas Sloan: Enlarged Methods for Discovering Knowledge

Whereas MacIntyre's improved university would initiate students into conflict and Schwehn's would initiate students into community characterized by spiritual virtues, Sloan's improved university would provide students and scholars with better methods and epistemologies informed by religious sensitivities and virtues. Douglas Sloan (2002) suggests that hopes for a more fruitful relationship between faith and knowledge lie in attempts to transform old modern epistemological assumptions. One change would be for qualitative ways of knowing to "lay claim to no less rigor, cogency, and necessity than the quantitative" (p. 23).

Sloan is particularly interested in qualitative ways of knowing nonsensory or supersensible realities often associated with religion. Although qualitative research has certainly made progress in the postmodern academy, Sloan makes the argument for the importance of religion in advancing new forms of qualitative knowledge. He cites Goethe's influence on what might be called a qualitative science of nature as an example. For Goethe, "the phenomena themselves carry their own meaning within them," and because "controlling concepts—in nature as in personal relationships—seldom leads to deeper understanding," so also "attention to the qualities of the phenomena can build capacities, new organs of cognition, for discerning qualitative reality and meaning" (Sloan, 2002, p. 33). Religious feelings such as reverence, Sloan believes, can aid in this sort of knowing. Echoing Schwehn, however, Sloan contends such forms of knowing require a radical transformation of ourselves. For example, "I can only come to know qualities in the world—the world of nature, the world of others, the world of the spiritual—to the extent that I can bring to birth and recognize those qualities in myself. The fruits of the Spirit—love, joy, peace, patience, and so forth—are non-sensory realities, but they are perceived and become realities for me only to the extent that I am able to identify with them and bring them to birth in myself. Such an inner transformation requires the participation of the whole human being—thinking, feeling, and willing" (pp. 33–34). Sloan maintains that developing such methodological virtues will also require that religion play an important role in our acquisition of genuine knowledge.

George Marsden: The Fair, Pragmatic Academy

Marsden's narrative in *The Outrageous Idea of Christian Scholarship* (1997) and his later essay, "Beyond Progressive Scientific Humanism" (2002), might be called the case for the fair, pragmatic academy. He mourns the secularization of scholarship and the failure of the secular academy to demonstrate what might be called "principled pluralism" in its sphere. In other words, the academy, while allowing worldview-based voices informed by feminism or Marxism, often fails to give religious worldviews and voices a hearing in academic debates. Here one finds Marsden's Reformed commitment to sphere sovereignty and principled pluralism.

Marsden suggests that if the broader academy is to be just and actually abide by a principled form of pluralism, it should realize that everyone presents worldview-informed scholarship and encourage a fair and just dialogue among the different participants without unfairly excluding some worldviews. To illustrate the situation for which Marsden longs, he cites the pragmatic university described by William James. James likens this academy to a corridor in a hotel: "Innumerable chambers open out of it. In one you may find a man writing an atheistic volume; in the next someone on his knees praying for faith and strength; in the third a chemist investigating a body's properties. In a fourth, a system of idealistic metaphysics is being excogitated; in a fifth the impossibility of metaphysics is being shown. But they all own the corridor, and all must pass through if they want a practicable way of getting into or out of their respective rooms" (1997, p. 46).

In other words, in an academy governed by pragmatic standards, no good reason exists to exclude religious perspectives or what he calls "faith-informed scholarship" (2002). Thus, just as one can be a feminist historian and narrate and evaluate history according to one's feminist commitment, the Christian historian whose scholarship is shaped by one's Christian commitments should also be given a place in the academy. In this respect, Marsden's hopeful future for a world of higher education that accepts a plurality of views and opinions at state or nonaffiliated private universities sounds quite similar to MacIntyre's approach.

Like MacIntyre, Marsden suggests that the whole system of higher education should contain a robust pluralism. Not only scholars but also universities should be able to be faith-informed institutions that seek to practice higher education in a distinct way. Thus, Marsden's hopeful vision also includes a wide variety of religious universities and colleges that support religious scholars. He points out that such colleges provide "a healthy alternative to the incoherence of much of the rest of the academy" (2002, p. 40). Most radical in his vision is his suggestion that "we have to recognize that our old assumptions about what constitutes progress should change" (p. 40). The bright future is not that represented by the secular research university but by a truly pluralistic academy.

C. John Sommerville: Enlarged Discourse in a Postsecular University

Sommerville's solution repeats much of what MacIntyre and Marsden suggest, although he offers more specific advice about how religion might help universities. Sommerville believes that moving from a secular to a postsecular university creates not merely the opportunity for the religious scholar and religious university in this situation but also the need for them. The reason is that they can help with a number of important questions.

One important question they can help answer is What does it mean to be fully human? Sommerville claims that universities must answer this question if they are to explain much of the way they function. "All of professional education, which absorbs the great majority of students today, depends on some particular understanding, even some ideal, of the human" (2006, p. 23). He believes, though, that the question can be adequately answered only by including religious discourse because conversations about the human only have "coherent meanings in a religious discourse" (p. 31). Naturalistic or secular discourse, he contends, while still hoping to discuss things like "truth," "freedom," "sanity," "responsibility," and "purpose," has difficulty doing so because these words are more at home in religious discourse. For example, he cites Polish philosopher Leszek Kolakowski's argument that the distinct status of humans disappears when the sacred disappears, which is why communist societies had no taboos about their treatment of humans. Sommerville claims religion can help with other questions: What is the soul? How should we judge between religions? How should we understand the distinction between fact and value?

Sommerville's ideal university is much like MacIntyre's and Marsden's vision, a place of extensive pluralism that is "incidentally secular in the sense that religion doesn't rule, but not officially secularist in the sense that religion is ruled out" (2006, p. 143). It would be a university that seeks "to understand all viewpoints that are able to win a hearing" and is "frank and relaxed about arguments over moral judgments" (2006, p. 143). Such universities would "openly acknowledge that humans are the most interesting things in creation, and make it their goal to explore the implications of this view" (2006, p. 143). They would also seek to help students know themselves rather than being alienated from their cultural background.

The Hope of Faith-Informed Narratives, Scholarship, and Universities

In the postmodern academy, one perhaps should not hope for too much consistency regarding diversity and justice. Nevertheless, it is the hope of those envisioning a new type of university. Not one of the scholars we mention hopes for a return to the older days of Christian hegemony. Moreover, not one of them supports reversing ecclesiastical secularization by having Christians gain power and favoritism through the power and funding of the state. These faith-informed commentators all believe that the future academy must be more pluralistic and more just with regard to addressing metaphysical or religious issues. "Since all enquiry and methods of enquiry are tradition-specific, all forms of education are sectarian in certain ways. There is no high ground in this debate, only differing forms of sectarianism, be they liberal, religious, feminist, psychoanalyst, and so on" (D'Costa, 2005, p. 217). Instead of dismissing or running scared from sectarianism, the academy must open its arms to it both professionally and institutionally. Such sentiment is perhaps one of the only shared sentiments among religious scholars. As a member of the National Lilly Seminar on Religion and Higher Education, Mark Schwehn found that "the group has reached consensus on almost nothing pertaining to the broad subject of the relationship between Christianity and the academy other than the view that institutional pluralism is a good thing for higher education" (2002a, p. 215).

Overall, what the religious visions in this chapter and other chapters offer is the particularly religious virtue of hope. In the closing essay of a volume discussing *The Future of Religious Colleges* (2002), Paul Dovre observes that one of the dominant themes of essayists was that of hopefulness, particularly in the area of religion and scholarship and religious higher education (p. 361). Certainly, if Nietzsche's Madman were to run into the marketplace during our era and shout "I seek God! I seek God!" he would perhaps receive more diverse answers than the one he originally received from his cultured despisers.

Perhaps the state of the contemporary situation is best represented by the recent debate at Harvard surrounding its core undergraduate curriculum. The Task Force on General Education initially recommended that students take a course on "reason and faith." Louis Menand, cochair of the committee, claimed the course would allow students to understand "rapid change and conflicts between reason and faith" (Bartlett, 2007, p. 10). The course received substantial resistance from various faculty, including the well-known professor of psychology Steven Pinker. In an op-ed piece in the *Harvard Crimson*, Pinker (2006) revealed that he still believed in a form of reason uninformed by a particular tradition or narrative. He wrote, "But universities are about reason, pure and simple. Faith—believing something without good reasons to do so—has no place in anything but a religious institution, and our society has no shortage of these" (p. A10). Undoubtedly, the writers and thinkers we have reviewed such as Alasdair MacIntyre, Nicholas Wolterstorff, and John Milbank would find Pinker's understanding of the relationship between faith and reason both modern and too simplistic. Perhaps the larger reason for Pinker's reticence, however, lies in his concern with giving religion too much attention in the tournament of narratives. He closed his letter by explaining, "For us to magnify the significance of religion as a topic equivalent in scope to all of science, all of culture, or all of world history and current affairs, is to give it far too much prominence. It is an American anachronism, I think, in an era in which the rest of the West is moving beyond it" (p. A10). Clearly for Pinker, the secularization narrative still not only provides historical fact but also prophetic precision.

Yet as the first chapter attempted to demonstrate, the inevitability of the secularization of scholarship and religious higher education has come under serious question. Against the currents of modern rationalism and scientism, a number of religious traditions have successfully nurtured alternative understandings of religiously formed rationality and scholarship. These traditions have helped nurture a growing conversation about the importance of faith-informed scholarship and influenced numerous scholars in various disciplines of the academy. Church-related universities and colleges are also attempting to put greater institutional efforts into the nurturing of scholars wishing to pursue faith-based research and writing that take both standards of the church and the academy seriously. Perhaps most telling of all, religious scholars are now writing their own more hopeful stories in the postmodern tournament of narratives. The hopefulness of the stories resides perhaps less in a belief about the circumstances surrounding religious scholarship in higher education than in a belief that religious scholars can find resources in a transcendent vision and being.

Interestingly, Harvard's committee decided, instead of offering a course addressing faith and reason, to offer a course addressing the issue of "what it means to be a human being." Even so, the course still raises issues related to religion, as John Sommerville (2006) observes: "If there is one thing that should raise the question of the secular university's irrelevance, it might especially be in the failure to justify or even make sense of the concept of the human" (p. 23). A discussion about what it means to be human, Sommerville claims, is more at home in religious discourse. If Sommerville is right, conversations about what it means to be human must still require attention to religiously informed discourse and scholarship. Perhaps it may still be the secular scholar of literature, Stanley Fish, who is a more accurate predictor of the importance of religion and God in the academy than Nietzsche.

References

After secularization. (2006). *Hedgehog Review, 8*(1&2).

Alford, H. J. (2006). *Rediscovering abundance: Interdisciplinary essays on wealth, income, and their distribution in the Catholic social tradition.* Notre Dame, IN: University of Notre Dame Press.

Alford, H. J., and Naughton, M. J. (2001). *Managing as if faith mattered: Christian social principles in the modern organization.* Notre Dame, IN: University of Notre Dame Press.

Ammerman, N. (2002). Sociology and the study of religion. In A. Sterk (Ed.), *Religion, scholarship, and higher education: Perspectives, models, and future prospects* (pp. 76–88). Notre Dame, IN: University of Notre Dame Press.

Asad, T. (2003). *Formations of the secular: Christianity, Islam, modernity.* Stanford, CA: Stanford University Press.

Association of Catholic Colleges and Universities Web site. Retrieved September 8, 2006, from http://www.accunet.org.

Astin, W. A., and Astin, H. S. (2006). *Spirituality and the professoriate: A national study of faculty beliefs, attitudes and behaviors.* Los Angeles: Higher Education Research Institute, University of California, Los Angeles.

Bartlett, T. (2007, January 5). Harvard drops religion requirement. *Chronicle of Higher Education, 53*(18), 10.

Bebbington, D. (1989). *Evangelicalism in modern Britain: A history from the 1730s to the 1890s.* London: Unwin Hyman.

Beiser, F. C. (2002). *German idealism: The struggle against subjectivism, 1781–1801.* Cambridge, MA: Harvard University Press.

Benne, R. (2001). *Quality with soul: How six premier colleges and universities keep faith with their religious traditions.* Grand Rapids, MI: Eerdmans.

Berger, P. L. (1967). *The sacred canopy: Elements of a sociological theory of religion.* Garden City, NY: Doubleday.

Berger, P. L. (1968). A bleak outlook is seen for religion. *New York Times,* 25 February, p. 3.

Best, H. M. (1993). *Music through the eyes of faith.* San Francisco: Harper.

Boyer, E. (1990). *Scholarship reconsidered: Priorities of the professoriate.* Princeton, NJ: Carnegie Foundation for the Advancement of Teaching.

Braskamp, L. A. (2007, Feb. 5). Fostering religious and spiritual development of students during college. Retrieved March 2007 from http://www.ssrc.org.

Braskamp, L. A., Trautvetter, L. C., and Ward, K. (2006). *Putting students first: How to develop students purposefully.* Bolton, MA: Anker.

Buchanan, J. M. (2007). Sound of Easter. *Christian Century, 124*(7), 3.

Buckley, M. J. (1998). *The Catholic university as promise and project.* Washington, DC: Georgetown University Press.

Burtchaell, J. T. (1998). *The dying of the light: The disengagement of the colleges and universities from their Christian churches.* Grand Rapids, MI: Eerdmans.

Calvin College Web site. Retrieved July 27, 2006, from http://www.calvin.edu.

Carpenter, J. A. (2002). The perils of prosperity: Neo-Calvinism and the future of religious colleges. In P. J. Dovre (Ed.), *The future of religious colleges: The proceedings of the Harvard conference on the future of religious colleges, October 6–7, 2000* (pp. 185–207). Grand Rapids, MI: Eerdmans.

Casanova, J. (1994). *Public religions in the modern world.* Chicago: University of Chicago Press.

Cavanaugh, W. T. (2004). Sailing under true colors: Academic freedom and the ecclesially based university. In M. Budde and J. Wright (Eds.), *Conflicting allegiances: The church-based university in a liberal democratic society* (pp. 31–52). Grand Rapids, MI: Brazos Press.

Chadwick, O. (1975). *The secularization of the European mind in the nineteenth century.* New York: Cambridge University Press.

Clouser, R. A. (2005). *The myth of religious neutrality: An essay on the hidden role of religious belief in theories.* Notre Dame, IN: University of Notre Dame Press.

Council for Christian Colleges and Universities. (2001). Enrollment continues to surge at Christian colleges. Retrieved May 21, 2007, from http://www.cccu.org/news/newsID.84, parentNAV.Archives/news_past_detail.asp.

Cramer, J. (1986). Academic freedom and the Catholic church. *Educational Record, 67*(2–3), 30–37.

Cuninggim, M. (1994). *Uneasy partners: The college and the church.* Nashville: Abingdon Press.

Curran, C. E. (1979). *Transition and tradition in moral theology.* Notre Dame, IN: University of Notre Dame Press.

Curran, C. E. (1980). Academic freedom: The Catholic university and Catholic theology. *Academe, 66*(3), 126–135.

Curran, C. E. (1982). *Moral theology: A continuing journey.* Notre Dame, IN: University of Notre Dame Press.

Curran, C. E. (1987). *Toward an American Catholic moral theology.* Notre Dame, IN: University of Notre Dame Press.

Curran, C. E. (1990). *Catholic higher education, theology, and academic freedom.* Notre Dame, IN: University of Notre Dame Press.

Curran, C. E. (1992). Church, academy, law: Personal reflections. In G. S. Worgul (Ed.), *Issues in academic freedom* (pp. 88–109). Pittsburgh: Duquesne University Press.

Dawkins, R. (2006). *The God delusion*. Boston: Houghton Mifflin.

D'Costa, G. (2005). *Theology in the public square: Church, academy and nation*. Malden, MA: Blackwell Publishing.

Diamond, J. (1999). *Guns, germs, and steel: The fates of human societies*. New York: W. W. Norton.

Diekema, A. J. (2000). *Academic freedom and Christian scholarship*. Grand Rapids, MI: Eerdmans.

Dovre, P. J. (Ed.). (2002). *The future of religious colleges*. Grand Rapids, MI: Eerdmans.

Dupré, L. (1993). *Passage to modernity: An essay in the hermeneutics of nature and culture*. New Haven, CT: Yale University Press.

Easton, L. D. (1957). Church-affiliated colleges and academic freedom. *Religion in Life, 26*(4), 544–549.

Edwards, M. U. (2006). *Religion on our campuses: A professor's guide to communities, conflicts, and promising conversations*. New York: Palgrave Macmillan.

Ericson, E. E. (1991). Academic freedom: Keeping it complex. A response to Samuel Logan. *Christian Scholar's Review, 21*(2), 182–190.

Fish, S. (1994). *There's no such thing as free speech . . . and it's a good thing, too*. New York: Oxford University Press.

Fish, S. (2003, January 23). Save the world on your own time. *Chronicle of Higher Education*. Retrieved January 23, 2005, from http://chronicle.com/jobs/2003/01/2003012301c.htm.

Fish, S. (2005, January 7). One university, under God? *Chronicle of Higher Education 51*, C1.

Fish, S. (2007, March 31). Religion without truth. *New York Times*, A27.

Fraser, D., and Campolo, T. (1992). *Sociology through the eyes of faith*. San Francisco: HarperCollins.

Gallagher, S., and Lundin, R. (1989). *Literature through the eyes of faith*. San Francisco: Harper & Row.

Gleason, P. (1987). *Keeping the faith: American Catholicism past and present*. Notre Dame, IN: University of Notre Dame Press.

Gleason, P. (1995). *Contending with modernity: Catholic higher education in the twentieth century*. New York: Oxford University Press.

Green, J. (2005). CCCU reports surging enrollment for Christian higher education. Retrieved June 29, 2006, from http://www.cccu.org/news/news_print.asp?type=pastand newsID=396.

Habecker, E. B. (1991). Academic freedom in the context of mission. *Christian Scholar's Review, 21*(2), 175–181.

Hatch, N. (1989). *The democratization of American Christianity*. New Haven, CT: Yale University Press.

Haughey, J. C. (Ed.). (2004). Revisiting the idea of vocation: Theological explorations. Washington, DC: Catholic University of America Press.

Hauser, M. (2006). *Moral minds: How nature designed our universal sense of right and wrong*. New York: Harper Collins.

Higher Education Research Institute, University of California, Los Angeles. (2006). Spirituality and the professoriate. Retrieved May 21, 2007, from http://www.spirituality. ucla.edu/results/spirit_professoriate.pdf#search=%22%22Spirituality%20and%20the%2 0Professoriate%22%20UCLA%22.

Hoekema, D. (1996). Politics, religion, and other crimes against civility. *Academe 82*(6), 33–37.

Hoff, C. (2004). Faith and learning: A dynamic restoration. *APU Life.* Azusa, CA: Azusa Pacific University.

Hofstadter, R., and Metzger, W. P. (1955). *The development of academic freedom in the United States.* New York: Columbia University Press.

Hollinger, D. A. (2002). Enough already: Universities do not need more Christianity. In A. Sterk (Ed.), *Religion, scholarship, and higher education: Perspectives, models, and future prospects.* Essays from the Lilly Seminar on religion and higher education (pp. 40–49). Notre Dame, IN: University of Notre Dame Press.

Hollinger, D. A. (2006). *Cosmopolitanism and solidarity: Studies in ethnoracial, religious, and professional affiliation in the United States.* Madison: University of Wisconsin Press.

Holmes, A. (1975). *The idea of a Christian college.* Grand Rapids: Eerdmans.

Holmes, A. (1977). *All truth Is God's truth.* Downers Grove, IL: Intervarsity.

Howard, T. A. (2000). *Religion and the rise of historicism: W.M.L. de Wette, Jacob Burckhardt, and the theological origins of nineteenth-century historical consciousness.* New York: Cambridge University Press.

Howard, T. A. (2006). *Protestant theology and the making of the modern German university.* New York: Oxford University Press.

Hoye, W. J. (1997). The religious roots of academic freedom. *Theological Studies, 58*(3), 409–428.

Hughes, R. T., and Adrian, W. B. (Eds.). (1997). *Models for Christian higher education: Strategies for success in the twenty-first century.* Grand Rapids, MI: Eerdmans.

Hunter, J. D. (1991). *Culture wars: The struggle to define America.* New York: Basic Books.

Huntington, S. P. (1996). *The clash of civilizations and the remaking of world order.* New York: Touchstone.

Jacobsen, D. G., and Jacobsen, R. H. (Eds.). (2004). *Scholarship and Christian faith: Enlarging the conversation.* New York: Oxford University Press.

Jencks, C., and Riesman, D. (2002/1968). *The academic revolution.* New Brunswick, NJ: Transaction Publishers.

John Paul II. (1990). *On Catholic universities: Ex corde ecclesiae.* Washington, DC: United States Catholic Conference.

Juhnke, J. C., and Hunter, C. M. (2001). *The missing peace: The search for nonviolent alternatives in United States history.* Kitchener, ON: Pandora Press.

Kaplan, C., and Schrecker, E. (1983). Regulating the intellectuals: Perspectives on academic freedom in the 1980s. Westport, CT: Praeger Publishers.

Kliever, L. D. (1988). Religion and academic freedom: Issues of faith and reason. *Academe, 74*(1), 8–11.

Kuhn, T. S. (1970). *The structure of scientific revolutions.* Chicago: University of Chicago Press.

Kuklick, B. (1996). Review of Marsden, *The soul of the American university. Method and Theory in the Study of Religion, 8*(1), 82.

Kuklick, B., and Hart, D. G. (1997). *Religious advocacy and American history.* Grand Rapids, MI: Eerdmans.

Kurland, J. E. (1986). Charles E. Curran: Theology professor at risk. *Academe, 72*(5), 43–44.

Kuyper, A. (1994). *Lectures on Calvinism.* Grand Rapids, MI: Eerdmans.

Lewis, H. R. (2006). *Excellence without a soul: How a great university forgot education.* New York: PublicAffairs.

Lilly Fellows Program in the Humanities and the Arts. Retrieved June 30, 2006, from http://www.lillyfellows.org.

Litfin, D. (2004). *Conceiving the Christian college.* Grand Rapids, MI: Eerdmans.

Logan, S. T. (1991). Academic freedom at Christian institutions. *Christian Scholar's Review, 21*(2), 164–174.

Long, D. S. (2000). *Divine economy: Theology and the market.* New York: Routledge.

Lundin, R. (1993). *The culture of interpretation: Christian faith and the postmodern world.* Grand Rapids, MI: Eerdmans.

Lundin, R. (1998). *Emily Dickinson and the art of belief.* Grand Rapids, MI: Eerdmans.

Lundin, R. (2005). *From nature to experience: The American search for cultural authority.* Lanham, MD: Rowman & Littlefield.

Lundin, R., Thiselton, A. C., and Walhout, C. (1985). *The responsibility of hermeneutics.* Grand Rapids, MI: Eerdmans.

Lundin, R., Walhout, C., and Thiselton, A. C. (1999). *The promise of hermeneutics.* Grand Rapids, MI: Eerdmans.

Lyon, L., and Beaty, M. (1999). Integration, secularization, and the two-spheres view at religious colleges: Comparing Baylor University with the University of Notre Dame and Georgetown College. *Christian Scholar's Review, 29*, 73–112.

Lyotard, J.-F. (1984). *The postmodern condition: A report on knowledge.* G. Bennington and B. Massumi (Trans.). Minneapolis: University of Minnesota Press.

MacIntyre, A. C. (1984). *After virtue: A study in moral theory.* Notre Dame, IN: University of Notre Dame Press.

MacIntyre, A. C. (1988). *Whose justice? Which rationality?* Notre Dame, IN: University of Notre Dame Press.

MacIntyre, A. C. (1990). *Three rival versions of moral enquiry: Encyclopaedia, genealogy and tradition.* Gifford lectures delivered in the University of Edinburgh in 1988. Notre Dame, IN: University of Notre Dame Press.

MacIntyre, A. C. (2006, October 20). The end of education: The fragmentation of the American university. *Commonweal, 10*–14.

Marquette University Web site. Retrieved July 13, 2006, from http://www.marquette.edu.

Marsden, G. M. (1980). *Fundamentalism and American culture: The shaping of twentieth-century evangelicalism, 1870–1925.* New York: Oxford University Press.

Marsden, G. M. (1993). The ambiguities of academic freedom. *Church History*, 62(2), 221–236.

Marsden, G. M. (1994). *The soul of the American university: From Protestant establishment to established nonbelief*. New York: Oxford University Press.

Marsden, G. M. (1997). *The outrageous idea of Christian scholarship*. New York: Oxford University Press.

Marsden, G. M. (1998, December). Liberating academic freedom. *First Things*, 88, 11–14.

Marsden, G. M. (2002). Beyond progressive scientific humanism. In P. J. Dovre (Ed.), *The future of religious colleges: The proceedings of the Harvard conference on the future of religious colleges, October 6–7, 2000* (pp. 35–50). Grand Rapids, MI: Eerdmans.

Marsden, G. M., and Longfield, B. J. (Eds.). (1992). *The secularization of the academy*. New York: Oxford University Press.

Martin, D. (1965). Towards eliminating the concept of secularization. In J. Gould (Ed.), *Penguin survey of the social sciences* (pp. 169–182). Harmondsworth, UK: Penguin Books.

Martin, D. (2005). *On secularization: Towards a revised general theory*. London: Ashgate.

May, W. W. (1988). Academic freedom in church-related institutions. *Academe*, 74(4), 23–28.

McClendon, J. W. (1986). *Ethics*. Nashville: Abingdon Press.

McConnell, M. W. (1993). Academic freedom in religious colleges and universities. In W. W. Van Alstyne (Ed.), *Freedom and tenure in the academy* (pp. 303–324). Durham, NC: Duke University Press.

McLeod, H. (2000). *Secularisation in western Europe, 1848–1914*. New York: St. Martin's Press.

Milbank, J. (1990). *Theology and social theory: Beyond secular reason*. Oxford: Blackwell.

Milbank, J., Ward, G., and Pickstock, C. (1999). *Radical orthodoxy: A new theology*. London: Routledge.

Moots, P. R., and Gaffney, E. M. (1979). *Church and campus, legal issues in religiously affiliated higher education*. Notre Dame, IN: University of Notre Dame Press.

Morey, M. M., and Piderit, J. J. (2006). *Catholic higher education: A culture in crisis*. New York: Oxford University Press.

Murphy, N. (1997). *Reconciling theology and science: A radical reformation perspective*. Kitchener, ON: Pandora Press.

Murphy, N. (2006). *Bodies and souls, or spirited bodies?* Cambridge: Cambridge University Press.

Murphy, N., and Ellis, G. (1996). *On the moral nature of the universe: Theology, cosmology, and ethics*. Minneapolis: Fortress Press.

Myers, D. G., and Jeeves, M. A. (2003). *Psychology: Through the eyes of faith*. New York: Harper.

Nash, R. J. (2001). *Religious pluralism in the academy: Opening the dialogue*. New York: Peter Lang.

Naugle, D. (2002). *Worldview: The history of a concept.* Grand Rapids, MI: Eerdmans.

Nichols, J. (1956). *History of Christianity, 1650–1950: Secularization of the West.* New York: Ronald Press.

Niebuhr, R. (1941). *The nature and destiny of man.* New York: Scribner's.

Nietzsche, F. (1882/1974). *The gay science.* New York: Vintage.

Noll, M. A. (1994). *The scandal of the evangelical mind.* Grand Rapids, MI: Eerdmans.

Noll, M. A. (2002). Teaching history as a Christian. In A. Sterk (Ed.), *Religion, scholarship, and higher education: Perspectives, models, and future prospects.* Essays from the Lilly Seminar on religion and higher education (pp. 161–171). Notre Dame, IN: University of Notre Dame Press.

Nuechterlein, J. (1993, December). The idol of academic freedom. *First Things, 38,* 12–16.

Nussbaum, M. C. (1997). *Cultivating humanity: A classical defense of reform in liberal education.* Cambridge, MA: Harvard University Press.

O'Brien, G. D. (2002). *The idea of a Catholic university.* Chicago: University of Chicago Press.

Parks, S. (2000). *Big questions, worthy dreams: Mentoring adults in the search for meaning, purpose, and faith.* San Francisco: Jossey-Bass.

Patterson, J. A. (2001). *Shining lights: A history of the Council for Christian Colleges and Universities.* Grand Rapids, MI: Baker Academic.

Pinker, S. (2006, October 27). Less faith, more reason. *Harvard Crimson,* A10.

Placher, W. C. (Ed.). (2005). *Callings: Twenty centuries of Christian wisdom on vocation.* Grand Rapids, MI: Eerdmans.

Plantinga, A. (1994). On Christian scholarship. In T. Hessburgh (Ed.), *The challenge and promise of a Catholic university* (pp. 267–296). Notre Dame: University of Notre Dame Press.

Plantinga, A. (2000). *Warranted Christian belief.* New York: Oxford University Press.

Poe, H. L. (2004). *Christianity in the academy: Teaching at the intersection of faith and learning.* Grand Rapids, MI: Baker Academic.

Polanyi, M. (2003). *Personal knowledge: Towards a post-critical philosophy.* London: Routledge.

Polkinghorne, J. C. (1998). *Belief in God in an age of science.* New Haven, CT: Yale University Press.

Polkinghorne, J. C. (2000). *Faith, science and understanding.* New Haven, CT: Yale University Press.

Polkinghorne, J. C. (2002). *The God of hope and the end of the world.* New Haven, CT: Yale University Press.

Polkinghorne, J. C. (2004). *Science and the trinity: The Christian encounter with reality.* New Haven, CT: Yale University Press.

Polkinghorne, J. C. (2005). *Exploring reality: The intertwining of science and religion.* New Haven, CT: Yale University Press.

Postman, N. (1995). *The end of education.* New York: Simon & Schuster.

Reuben, J. (1996). *The making of the modern university: Intellectual transformation and the marginalization of morality.* Chicago: University of Chicago Press.

Riley, N. S. (2005). *God on the quad: How religious colleges and the missionary generation are changing America.* New York: St. Martin's Press.

Ringenberg, W. (2006). *The Christian college: A history of Protestant higher education in America.* Grand Rapids, MI: Baker Academic.

Roberts, J., and Turner, J. (2000). *The sacred and the secular university.* Princeton, NJ: Princeton University Press.

Roche, M. W. (2003). *The intellectual appeal of Catholicism and the idea of a Catholic university.* Notre Dame, IN: University of Notre Dame.

Rorty, R. (1999). *Philosophy and social hope.* New York: Penguin Books.

Rüegg, W. (1992). Themes. In H. D. Ridder-Symeons (Ed.), *A history of the university in Europe, Vol. 1.* New York: Cambridge University Press.

Russell, B. (1957). *Why I am not a Christian, and other essays on religion and related subjects.* New York: Simon & Schuster.

Sawatsky, R. (1997). What can the Mennonite tradition contribute to Christian higher education? In R. T. Hughes and W. B. Adrian (Eds.), *Models for Christian higher education: Strategies in the twenty-first century* (pp. 187–199). Grand Rapids, MI: Eerdmans.

Sawatsky, R. (2004). Prologue: The virtue of scholarly hope. In D. Jacobsen and R. H. Jacobsen (Eds.), *Scholarship and Christian faith: Enlarging the conversation* (pp. 3–14). New York: Oxford University Press.

Schultz, K. M. (2006). Secularization: A bibliographic essay. *Hedgehog Review, 8*(1–2), 170–178.

Schultze, Q. J. (2005). *Here I am: Now what on Earth should I be doing?* Grand Rapids, MI: Baker Books.

Schwehn, M. (2002a). Lutheran higher education in the twenty-first century. In P. J. Dovre (Ed.), *The future of religious colleges: The proceedings of the Harvard conference on the future of religious colleges, October 6–7, 2000* (pp. 208–223). Grand Rapids, MI: Eerdmans.

Schwehn, M. (2002b). Where are the universities of tomorrow? In A. Sterk (Ed.), *Religion, scholarship, and higher education: Perspectives, models, and future prospects.* Essays from the Lilly Seminar on religion and higher education (pp. 50–59). Notre Dame, IN: University of Notre Dame Press.

Schwehn, M. C., and Bass, D. C. (Eds.). (2006). *Leading lives that matter: What we should do and who we should be.* Grand Rapids, MI: Eerdmans.

Schwehn, M. R. (1993). *Exiles from Eden: Religion and the academic vocation in America.* New York: Oxford University Press.

Simon, C. J., Bloxham, L., and Doyle, D. (2003). *Mentoring for mission: Nurturing new faculty at church-related colleges.* Grand Rapids, MI: Eerdmans.

Skillen, J. W., and McCarthy, R. M. (1991). *Political order and the plural structure of society.* Atlanta: Scholars Press.

Sloan, D. (1994). *Faith and knowledge: Mainline Protestantism and American higher education.* Louisville, KY: Westminster/John Knox Press.

126

Sloan, D. (2002). Faith and knowledge: Religion and the modern university. In P. J. Dovre (Ed.), *The future of religious colleges: The proceedings of the Harvard conference on the future of religious colleges, October 6–7, 2000* (pp. 3–35). Grand Rapids, MI: Eerdmans.

Smith, C. (2003). *The secular revolution: Power, interests, and conflict in the secularization of American public life.* Berkeley: University of California Press.

Smith, J. (2004). *Introducing radical orthodoxy.* Grand Rapids, MI: Baker Academic.

Sommerville, C. J. (1998, June). Secular society/religious population: Our tacit rules for using the term "secularization." *Journal for the Scientific Study of Religion, 37,* 249–253.

Sommerville, C. J. (2006). *The decline of the secular university.* New York: Oxford University Press.

Stark, R. (1999). Secularization, R.I.P. *Sociology of Religion, 60*(3), 249–273.

Stark, R. (2001). *One true God: The historical consequences of monotheism.* Princeton, NJ: Princeton University Press.

Stark, R. (2003). *For the glory of God: How monotheism led to reformations, science, witch hunts, and the end of slavery.* Princeton, NJ: Princeton University Press.

Stark, R. (2005). *The victory of reason: How Christianity led to freedom, capitalism, and western success.* New York: Random House.

Sterk, A. (Ed.). (2002). *Religion, scholarship, and higher education: Perspectives, models, and future prospects.* Essays from the Lilly Seminar on religion and higher education. Notre Dame, IN: University of Notre Dame Press.

Swatos, W. H., and Christiano, K. J. (2000). Secularization theory: The course of a concept. In W. H. Swatos and D. Olson (Eds.), *The secularization debate* (pp. 1–20). Lanham, MD: Rowman & Littlefield.

Swatos, W. H., and Olson, D., eds. (2000). *The secularization debate.* Lanham, MD: Rowman & Littlefield Publishers.

Taylor, C. (1989). *Sources of the self: The making of the modern identity.* Cambridge, MA: Harvard University Press.

Turner, J. (2002). Does religion have anything worth saying to scholars? In A. Sterk (Ed.), *Religion, scholarship, and higher education: Perspectives, models, and future prospects.* Essays from the Lilly Seminar on religion and higher education (pp. 16–21). Notre Dame, IN: University of Notre Dame Press.

Turner, J. (2003). *Language, religion, knowledge: Past and present.* Notre Dame, IN: University of Notre Dame Press.

Van Till, H. J. (1986). *The fourth day: What the Bible and the Heavens are telling us about the Creation.* Grand Rapids, MI: Publishing Company.

Villanova University Web site. Retrieved July 13, 2006, from http://www.villanova.edu.

Wagner, K. (2006). Faith statements do restrict academic freedom: Most defenses of evangelical colleges miss the point. *Academe, 92*(1), 21–22.

Walton, C. C. (1990). Academic freedom at the Catholic University of America during the 1970s. *Catholic Historical Review, 76*(3), 555–563.

Ward, G. (2000). *Cities of God.* New York: Routledge.

Weaver-Zercher, D. L. (2002). *Minding the church: Scholarship in the Anabaptist tradition. Essays in honor of E. Morris Sider.* Telford, PA: Pandora Press.

Weaver-Zercher, D. L. (2004). A modest (though not particularly humble) claim for scholarship in the Anabaptist tradition. In D. Jacobsen and R. H. Jacobsen (Eds.), *Scholarship and Christian faith: Enlarging the conversation* (pp. 103–117). New York: Oxford University Press.

Wells, R. A. (1989). *History through the eyes of faith.* San Francisco: Harper.

Wheaton College. (2006). Private access Web site. Retrieved July 14, 2006, from www.wheaton.edu.

White, A. D. (1955). *A history of the warfare of science with theology in Christendom.* New York: George Braziller.

Wilcox, J. R., and King, I. (Eds.). (2000). *Enhancing religious identity.* Washington, DC: Georgetown University Press.

Williams, C. (2002). *The life of the mind: A Christian perspective.* Grand Rapids, MI: Baker Academic.

Williams, D. D. (1953). Christian freedom and academic freedom. *The Christian Scholar, 36*(1), 11–22.

Witham, L. (1991). *Curran vs. Catholic university: A study of authority and freedom in conflict.* Riverdale, MD: Edington-Rand.

Wolfe, A. (2000, October). The opening of the evangelical mind. *Atlantic Monthly, 55*–76.

Wolfe, A. (2004). Scholars infuse religion with cultural light. *Chronicle of Higher Education, 51*(9), 6.

Wolterstorff, N. (1976). *Reason within the bounds of religion.* Grand Rapids, MI: Eerdmans.

Wolterstorff, N. (1989). *Keeping faith: Talks for new faculty at Calvin College.* Grand Rapids, MI: Calvin College.

Wolterstorff, N. (1999). *Reason within the bounds of religion.* Rev. ed. Grand Rapids, MI: Eerdmans.

Wright, R. T. (2003). *Biology through the eyes of faith.* (rev. ed.). San Francisco: Harper.

Wuthnow, R. (1989). *The struggle for America's soul: Evangelicals, liberals and secularism.* Grand Rapids, MI: Eerdmans.

Wuthnow, R. (1996a). *Christianity and civil society: The contemporary debate.* Valley Forge, PA: Trinity Press International.

Wuthnow, R. (1996b). *Poor Richard's principle: Recovering the American dream through the moral dimension of work, business, and money.* Princeton, NJ: Princeton University Press.

Wuthnow, R. (1998). *After heaven: Spirituality in America since the 1950s.* Berkeley: University of California Press.

Wuthnow, R. (1999). *Growing up religious: Christians and Jews and their journeys of faith.* Boston: Beacon Press.

Wuthnow, R. (2001). *Creative spirituality: The way of the artist.* Berkeley: University of California Press.

Wuthnow, R. (2003). *All in sync: How music and art are revitalizing American religion.* Berkeley: University of California Press.

Wuthnow, R. (2005). *America and the challenges of religious diversity.* Princeton, NJ: Princeton University Press.

Yoder, J. H. (1984). *The priestly kingdom: Social ethics as gospel.* Notre Dame, IN: University of Notre Dame Press.

Zagano, P. (1990). Sectarian universities, federal funding and the question of academic freedom. *Religious Education, 85*(1), 136–148.

Name Index

A
Adrian, W. B., 72, 74
Alford, H. J., 54
Ammerman, N., 52, 59
Aquinas, T., 11, 29, 32, 34, 90
Asad, T., 21
Astin, H. S., 10
Astin, W. A., 10
Augustine, 28, 34, 56

B
Bach, J. S., 58
Bartlett, T., 117
Barzun, J., 103
Bass, D., 76
Beaty, M., 16
Bebbington, D., 10
Beiser, F. C., 12
Benne, R., 15, 16, 27, 37, 40, 66, 72, 73, 74, 75
Berger, P., 9, 20, 21, 50
Berlin, I., 93
Best, H. M., 69
Bloxham, L., 75
Bohm, D., 58
Bohr, N., 58
Boyer, E., 3
Braskamp, L. A., 73
Buckley, M. J., 32
Burtchaell, J., 8, 17, 18, 21, 25, 35, 65

C
Calvin, J., 35, 98
Campolo, T., 59
Carpenter, J., 11, 29, 35, 36, 37
Casanova, J., 8, 17, 22
Cavanaugh, W. T., 92, 93, 94, 95
Chadwick, O., 9
Christiano, K., 21
Clouser, R. A., 47, 50, 52, 53
Comte, A., 20
Cramer, J., 96
Cunninggim, M., 10
Curran, C. E., 96–97, 99
Custer, G., 44

D
Darwin, C., 18, 19
Dawkins, R., 102
D'Costa, G., 100, 116
Derrida, J., 1, 24
Descartes, R., 103
Dewey, J., 92, 93, 108
Diamond, J., 61, 62, 63
Diekema, A. J., 84, 85, 98, 99
Dovre, P., 2, 20, 47, 72, 117
Doyle, D., 75
Dupré, L., 13
Dwight, T., 11

E
Easton, L. D., 85
Edwards, J., 10, 11

Edwards, M. U., vii, 15, 27, 47, 52
Ellis, G., 42, 43
Emerson, R. W., 62
Engels, F., 20
Ericson, E. E., 85
Evans, C. S., 76

F

Fichte, J. G., 12
Fish, S., 1, 2, 92, 94, 95, 118
Foucault, M., 24
Fraser, D., 59

G

Gaffney, E. M., 85
Gallagher, S., 52, 62
Gleason, P., 11, 17, 29, 30
Goethe, J. W., 113
Green, J., 4

H

Habecker, E. B., 85, 86
Hart, D. G., 50
Hatch, N., 14
Haughey, J. C., 76
Hauser, M., 51, 63
Hegel, G.W.F., 13
Hickey, J. A., 97
Hoekema, D., 85
Hoff, C., 77
Hofstadter, R., 87, 88, 89, 91
Hollinger, D., 50, 52
Holmes, A., 40
Howard, T. A., 12, 13, 14, 25
Hoye, W. J., 89, 90
Hughes, R. T., 72, 74
Hunter, C., 42
Hunter, J. D., 67
Huntington, S. P., 102

J

Jacobsens, D. G. and R. H., 3, 32, 40, 42,
  43, 44, 47, 49, 50, 51, 52, 53, 66
James, W., 114
Jeeves, M., 47, 49, 50, 51, 52, 53, 54

Jencks, C., 3, 4, 21
Juhnke, J., 42

K

Kant, I., 12, 38
Kaplan, C., 84
King, I., 32
Kliever, L. D., 85
Kohlberg, L., 55
Kolakowski, L., 115
Kuhn, T., 48
Kuklick, B., 27, 28, 44, 50
Kurland, J. E., 96, 97
Kuyper, A., 35, 36, 37, 41

L

Lewis, H. R., 102, 106
Litfin, D., 40, 75, 85
Logan, S. T., 85
Long, D. S., 24
Longfield, B. J., 8, 21
Lundin, R., 52, 61–63, 79
Lyon, L., 16
Lyotard, J-F., 4, 101, 102

M

MacIntyre, A., 31, 33, 34, 103, 104, 105,
  106, 107, 109, 110, 111–112, 113, 114,
  115, 116, 117
Marsden, G., 7, 8, 9, 13, 14, 15, 17, 21,
  22, 27, 35, 38, 39, 40, 44, 47, 49, 50,
  51, 52, 53, 54, 62, 63, 65, 66, 79, 89,
  90, 91, 108–109, 114–115, 116
Martin, D., 20
May, W. W., 85
McCarthy, R. M., 36
McClendon, J., 102
McConnell, M. W., 85
McLeod, H., 23
Menand, L., 117
Metzger, W. P., 87, 88, 89, 91
Milbank, J., 23, 24, 59, 60, 63, 79, 117
Miller, P., 52
Moots, P. R., 85
Morey, M. M., 17, 30, 32, 33, 76

Subject Index

A
Academic freedom
  defining, 84–86
  history of faith-informed scholarship
    and, 87–91
  individual scholars on, 92–95
  institutional examples of, 95–100
Academic vocation
  corruption of, 106–107
  help for restoring, 112
Agendas and motivations, scholarly,
    49–50
American Association of University
  Professors (AAUP), 85, 88, 89, 90, 91,
    92, 93
Anabaptist narrative, 40–43, 44
Association for Jesuit Colleges and
  Universities (AJCU), 66–67
Association of Catholic Colleges and
  Universities, 66

B
Background beliefs
  agendas and, 49–50
  data to be studied and, 51–52
  interpretive task and, 52–54
  method to obtain knowledge and,
    50–51
  moral evaluation of results and, 54–55
  overall influence of, 55–57
  six areas influenced by, 48–49

C
Calvin College, 27, 37, 44, 71, 77–78, 96,
    97–99
Catholic doctrine and secularization in
  Catholic colleges, 16–17, 18
Catholic tradition of faith-informed
  scholarship, 28–35, 44
On Catholic Universities: Ex Corde Ecclesiae,
    30–32
Catholic University of America (CUA),
    96–97
Choice of data or phenomena to study,
    49, 51–52
Christian professional associations, 79,
    80–81
Control beliefs, 39
Council for Christian Colleges and
  Universities (CCCU), 4, 40,
    67–69

D
Darwin's theory of origins, 19
Data beliefs, 39
Data or phenomena, identification of
  important, 49, 51–52
Data-background beliefs, 39

E
Evangelical Protestantism, 10–11,
    13, 14
Ex Corde, 30–32

F

Faith and Knowledge: Mainline Protestantism and American Higher Education, 15

Faith-informed scholarship
  Anabaptist outlook, 40–43
  Catholic tradition of, 28–35
  Reformed tradition of, 35–40

False prophet, Nietzsche as, 1–2

Fundamentalism, 14

H

Harvard University, 10, 13, 87, 106, 117, 118

Hiring for religious and scholarly mission, 73–75

Historical influence of faith-informed or atheist-informed scholarship, 55–57

Hope, religious virtue of, 117

Humanities and religion, 61–63

I

Identity crisis in Catholic schools, 30

Interpretive task, 49, 52–54

K

Knowledge
  enlarged methods for discovering, 113
  limits of modern, 107–108

L

Laypeople in Catholic colleges, 30

Liberal university, irrationality and fragmentation of, 103–105

Lilly Fellows Program in Humanities and the Arts (LFP), 69–71

M

Mennonite colleges, 40–43

Mentoring programs, 75–77

Method to obtain knowledge, choice of, 49, 50–51

Methodological naturalism, 18–19, 20

Moral evaluation of results, 49, 54–55

N

Narratives of hope for postsecular university, 110–116

Narratives on demise of secular university, 101–110

Neo-Thomism, 29, 30

Networks of religious colleges and universities, 66–71

Networks of scholars and professional associations, 79–81

O

Outrageous Idea of Christian Scholarship, The, 7

P

Philological historicism, 18, 19

Postliberal university, the, 111–112

Postsecular university, narratives of hope for, 110–116

Princeton University, 10, 11, 13

Principled pluralism, 114–115

Professional associations, Christian, 79, 80–81

Progressive scientific humanism, demise of, 108–109

Promotion and tenure, 77–78

Protestant denominational networks, 67

Protestantism, evangelical, 10–11, 13, 14

R

Radical orthodoxy, 24–25

Reason and faith, 117

Reformed tradition of faith-informed scholarship, 35–40, 44

Religion and practices of an institution
  eight aspects of, 72
  hiring, 73–75
  mentoring, 75–77
  promotion and tenure, 77–78
  support structures, 78–79

Religion on Our Campuses, 15

Religious roots of higher education, 10–12

About the Authors

Todd C. Ream is the associate director of the John Wesley Honors College and assistant professor of Humanities at Indiana Wesleyan University. He received a B.A. in Religion from Baylor University, a M.Div. from Duke University Divinity School, and a Ph.D. in Higher Education from The Pennsylvania State University. Prior to coming to Indiana Wesleyan, he served as a postdoctoral research fellow (Baylor University), a dean of students (Oklahoma Baptist University), and a residence director (Messiah College). His teaching and research interests include philosophical and theological explorations of the curricular and co-curricular efforts of colleges and universities. His scholarly articles have appeared in journals such as *Christian Scholar's Review, Educational Philosophy and Theory,* the *Journal of General Education,* and *New Blackfriars.* This volume is his first book-length project.

Perry L. Glanzer is associate professor in the School of Education at Baylor University. He received his B.A. in Religion, History, and Political Science from Rice University, an M.A. in Church-State Studies from Baylor University, and his Ph.D. in Social Ethics from the University of Southern California. His teaching and research interests include the relationship between religion and education, the study of moral education, and the relationship of both religious and moral education to politics. His scholarly work addresses these topics in both the United States and the former Soviet Union with his first book, *The Quest for Russia's Soul: Evangelicals and Moral Education in Post-Communist Russia* (Baylor University Press), covering this topic in the Russian context. His scholarly articles have appeared in journals such as *Christian Scholar's Review,* the *Journal of General Education,* the *Journal of Church and State,* and the *Journal of Moral Education.*

About the ASHE Higher Education Report Series

Since 1983, the ASHE (formerly ASHE-ERIC) Higher Education Report Series has been providing researchers, scholars, and practitioners with timely and substantive information on the critical issues facing higher education. Each monograph presents a definitive analysis of a higher education problem or issue, based on a thorough synthesis of significant literature and institutional experiences. Topics range from planning to diversity and multiculturalism, to performance indicators, to curricular innovations. The mission of the Series is to link the best of higher education research and practice to inform decision making and policy. The reports connect conventional wisdom with research and are designed to help busy individuals keep up with the higher education literature. Authors are scholars and practitioners in the academic community. Each report includes an executive summary, review of the pertinent literature, descriptions of effective educational practices, and a summary of key issues to keep in mind to improve educational policies and practice.

The Series is one of the most peer reviewed in higher education. A National Advisory Board made up of ASHE members reviews proposals. A National Review Board of ASHE scholars and practitioners reviews completed manuscripts. Six monographs are published each year and they are approximately 120 pages in length. The reports are widely disseminated through Jossey-Bass and John Wiley & Sons, and they are available online to subscribing institutions through Wiley InterScience (http://www.interscience.wiley.com).

Call for Proposals

The ASHE Higher Education Report Series is actively looking for proposals. We encourage you to contact one of the editors, Dr. Kelly Ward (kaward@wsu.edu) or Dr. Lisa Wolf-Wendel (lwolf@ku.edu), with your ideas.

Christian Faith and Scholarship

Recent Titles

ASHE HIGHER EDUCATION REPORT
Order Form
SUBSCRIPTIONS AND SINGLE ISSUES

DISCOUNTED BACK ISSUES:

Use this form to receive **20% off** all back issues of ASHE Higher Education Report. All single issues priced at **$22.40** (normally $28.00)

TITLE	ISSUE NO.	ISBN
_____	_____	_____
_____	_____	_____

Call 888-378-2537 or see mailing instructions below. When calling, mention the promotional code, JB7ND, to receive your discount.

SUBSCRIPTIONS: *(1 year, 6 issues)*

☐ New Order   ☐ Renewal

U.S.	☐ Individual: $165	☐ Institutional: $199
Canada/Mexico	☐ Individual: $165	☐ Institutional: $235
All Others	☐ Individual: $201	☐ Institutional: $310

Call 888-378-2537 or see mailing and pricing instructions below. Online subscriptions are available at www.interscience.wiley.com.

Copy or detach page and send to:
John Wiley & Sons, Journals Dept., 5th Floor
989 Market Street, San Francisco, CA 94103-1741
Order Form can also be faxed to: 888-481-2665

Issue/Subscription Amount: $ _____
Shipping Amount: $ _____
(for single issues only—subscription prices include shipping)
Total Amount: $ _____

SHIPPING CHARGES:

SURFACE	Domestic	Canadian
First Item	$5.00	$6.00
Each Add'l Item	$3.00	$1.50

(No sales tax for U.S. subscriptions. Canadian residents, add GST for subscription orders. Individual rate subscriptions must be paid by personal check or credit card. Individual rate subscriptions may not be resold as library copies.)

☐ Payment enclosed (U.S. check or money order only. All payments must be in U.S. dollars.)

☐ VISA ☐ MC ☐ Amex # _____ Exp. Date_____

Card Holder Name _____ Card Issue # _____

Signature_____ Day Phone _____

☐ Bill Me (U.S. institutional orders only. Purchase order required.)

Purchase order # _____
Federal Tax ID13559302   GST 89102 8052

Name_____

Address _____

Phone _____ E-mail _____

JB7ND

ASHE-ERIC HIGHER EDUCATION REPORT IS NOW AVAILABLE ONLINE AT WILEY INTERSCIENCE

What is Wiley InterScience?

Wiley InterScience is the dynamic online content service from John Wiley & Sons delivering the full text of over 300 leading scientific, technical, medical, and professional journals, plus major reference works, the acclaimed Current Protocols laboratory manuals, and even the full text of select Wiley print books online.

What are some special features of Wiley InterScience?

Wiley Interscience Alerts is a service that delivers table of contents via e-mail for any journal available on Wiley InterScience as soon as a new issue is published online.

Early View is Wiley's exclusive service presenting individual articles online as soon as they are ready, even before the release of the compiled print issue. These articles are complete, peer-reviewed, and citable.

CrossRef is the innovative multi-publisher reference linking system enabling readers to move seamlessly from a reference in a journal article to the cited publication, typically located on a different server and published by a different publisher.

How can I access Wiley InterScience?

Visit http://www.interscience.wiley.com.

Guest Users can browse Wiley InterScience for unrestricted access to journal Tables of Contents and Article Abstracts, or use the powerful search engine.

Registered Users are provided with a *Personal Home Page* to store and manage customized alerts, searches, and links to favorite journals and articles. Additionally, Registered Users can view free Online Sample Issues and preview selected material from major reference works.

Licensed Customers are entitled to access full-text journal articles in PDF, with select journals also offering full-text HTML.

How do I become an Authorized User?

Authorized Users are individuals authorized by a paying Customer to have access to the journals in Wiley InterScience. For example, a University that subscribes to Wiley journals is considered to be the Customer.

Faculty, staff and students authorized by the University to have access to those journals in Wiley InterScience are Authorized Users. Users should contact their Library for information on which Wiley journals they have access to in Wiley InterScience.

ASK YOUR INSTITUTION ABOUT WILEY INTERSCIENCE TODAY!